MANAGING
THE MEDIA

Recent Titles from Quorum Books

MANAGING THE MEDIA

PROACTIVE STRATEGY FOR BETTER BUSINESS-PRESS RELATIONS

FRED J. EVANS

Q QUORUM BOOKS

NEW YORK • WESTPORT, CONNECTICUT • LONDON

Library of Congress Cataloging-in-Publication Data

Evans, Fred J.
  Managing the media.

  Bibliography: p.
  Includes index.
  1. Public relations. 2. Press releases.
3. Journalism, Commercial. I. Title.
HD59.E93 1987   659.2   86-25736
ISBN 0-89930-156-8 (lib. bdg. : alk. paper)

Library of Congress Catalog Card Number: 86-25736
ISBN: 0-89930-156-8

First published in 1987 by Quorum Books

Greenwood Press, Inc.
88 Post Road West, Westport, Connecticut 06881

Printed in the United States of America

The paper used in this book complies with the
Permanent Paper Standard issued by the National
Information Standards Organization (Z39.48-1984).

10 9 8 7 6 5 4 3 2 1

Contents

Illustrations

Tables

Acknowledgments

I wish to thank my graduate assistants David Marchant and Sue Shochat for their help on the case studies. Dave worked especially hard gathering data on BKK Corporation. I also would like to thank Nedra West, editor of *Business Forum*, for reviewing the manuscript for form and content; her comments were invaluable. Bobbi Villalobos' editorial and indexing assistance was greatly appreciated. I am also thankful to Irene Jaimes for providing fast and accurate clerical help.

Errors of commission or ommission should, of course, be attributed to Sue, David, Nedra, Bobbi, or Irene. The author takes sole responsibility for whatever is found to be original or enlightening.

Chapter 2 is a slightly modified version of Fred J. Evans, "The Politics of the Press," *Business Horizons*, Vol. 27, No. 2 (March/ April 1984); Chapter 3 is a greatly expanded version of Fred J. Evans, "Business and the Press: Conflicts Over Roles, Fairness," *Public Relations Review*, Vol. X, No. 4 (Winter, 1984); Chapter 4 is a modified version of Fred J. Evans, "Business: Attacked from Without and Undermined from Within?," *IPRA Review*, Vol. 7, No. 3 (November, 1983); the appendix to Chapter 3 is adapted from my review of *Ninety Seconds to Tell it All*, by A. Kent MacDougall, *Policy Review*, Vol. 21 (Summer, 1982).

Introduction

MANIPULATE THE PRESS!

This book is based on the controversial if not heretical notion that business should attempt to manipulate the press in order to accomplish its objectives and defend its interests. Such a statement will appear sinister—even Machiavellian—to many public relations professionals, not to mention journalists. The view of many public relations professionals, especially those who think themselves at the forefront of the field, is that business ought to be open with the press whenever possible and that there should never be an attempt to manipulate or deceive. The greatest fear is that management will be advised exclusively by attorneys, and their typically cautious message will be "no comment." Not to be open with the press is said to court press hostility and suspicion. Such a strategy also is said to be futile: the press will get the story anyway, most likely from hostile sources.

Being open and honest with the press is a way of developing good press relations, these professionals contend. Journalists, like everybody else, have a job to do, and if you facilitate their work by telling them what they want to know, they will return the courtesy with cooperation. The fruits of an open and honest press strategy will be better press relations and better (more favorable) news coverage.

This admittedly oversimplifies the position of these public relations executives. The simplification is instructive, however. Although public relations professionals represent business (or other clients), they are also intermediaries between business and the press. They want not only to effectively communicate the company's message but also to please the press. (A policy of open and honest press relations can be good PR.) Journalists have a vested interest in information, and the more open their contacts are, the easier their job. Thus, as a philosophy, openness and honesty with the press always will meet with enthusiastic support from journalists.

The argument of this book is not that business should not communicate with the press. On the contrary, I strongly believe that business, particularly big business, has become a quasi-public institution with special responsibilities beyond profit maximization. One of the most important of these responsibilities is public communication.

There are a variety of ways for a company to communicate to the public, from employee and shareholder newsletters to special customer relations activities to advertising. However, a major channel of public communication is through the news media, and to effectively communicate a company's interests to the public through the news media is the best public relations of all. The problem is that this channel is subject to great and pervasive distortion. To naively pursue a strategy of openness and honesty is to do nothing to correct this distortion.

Thus, the primary purpose of this book is to help the reader understand how this distortion occurs so he can use the knowledge to devise a press strategy that will overcome or minimize it. If the object is to present the company's message to the public with as little distortion as possible, the press must be manipulated. The best press strategy will not be the most highly acclaimed by the press, its primary concern will not be how to make the journalist's job easier, and it will not be a policy of total openness or even total honesty. Sometimes—but not always—it will be a strategy of partial openness and incomplete disclosure of facts. The strategy will be tailored to the particular company and situation and the primary concern will be to minimize distortion.

THE CHANGING BUSINESS CLIMATE

Effective communication to the public through the press is difficult at best. Unfortunately, the stakes are high and getting higher.

Changes that have occurred in the business climate in the last two decades explain why this communication effort is so urgent.

American business exists at the pleasure of American public opinion. Period. This proposition is supported in theory and historical experience. It should be burned into the consciousness of every business executive in America. Unfortunately, the proposition will strike many business executives (and a not inconsiderable number of academics) as either false or trivial.

After all, are not the chief executives of large companies barely constrained by their board of directors and stockholders, much less something as nebulous as public opinion? Although most day-to-day decisions are remote from public consciousness and concern, the sum of all of these day-to-day decisions, both major and minor, will ultimately be judged at the bar of public opinion. This judgment, as it occurs through time, will chart the course for American business.

Ignorance and complacency on the part of American business leaders is the principal danger to the future of American business. If day-to-day business decisions are viewed in exclusively economic terms, the longer run and more subtle implications of these decisions on public opinion will be ignored. Granted, the short-term, economic bias in decision making is difficult to overcome: the executive who does not make economically successful decisions will fail. Thus, the sole question often appears to be whether or not the economically correct decision has or has not been made. The real test of a decision, however, is whether it is economically viable in the long run. In contemporary American society this includes passing the test of public opinion.

A recent *Wall Street Journal* article described how a young stockbroker became phenomenally successful by reaping commissions made from investing his uncle's fortune. In the long run the would-be wonder boy failed because the investments lost money. This was an obvious case of short-run success and long-run failure. However, how much difference is there between this example of failure and that of a utility which decides on economic grounds that construction of a nuclear power plant will be profitable without considering possible adverse public reaction? Of course, everyone in the industry now understands the political risks associated with the construction of nuclear generating plants, but why not 10 or 15 years ago when construction began? At least a partial answer is that the customary narrow economic focus of decision making is responsible for this and similar costly oversights. By paying more attention to long-run, noneconomic implications of decisions many of these errors could be avoided.

Complacency also results from the historical security of American business. In virtually every other industrial nation in the world, business has had less independence and has been subordinated more capriciously to the purposes of politics and politicians than American business. In the United States, nationalization of the economy preceded nationalization of the polity, and in the twentieth century the United States became a political power by virtue of its economic power. As the primary engine of the economy, business has enjoyed relative prestige and autonomy. Opinion polls consistently show that not only does the public oppose nationalization of industry, most people do not even have a clear concept of what socialism is.

The fact is that the legitimacy of private enterprise is more firmly established in the public consciousness in the United States than in any other industrialized country. This has led to the view among many executives that private enterprise is somehow divinely inspired —unchallenged and unchallengeable. This view courts disaster. In country after country private enterprise has come under attack, and even in the United States public opinion has turned sharply critical of business in the last two decades. Private enterprise is everywhere vulnerable to attack because it is counterintuitive. The private enterprise economy, where the economic decisions of millions of individuals are coordinated by the "invisible hand" of the marketplace to the benefit of the consuming public, is an enormously sophisticated notion that must be explained and justified again and again. The complacency of American business undermines this vitally essential process of explanation and justification.

PUBLIC OPINION IS PARAMOUNT

To return to a central proposition of this book: American private enterprise depends for its existence on the support of the American public. To assure its continued viability, American business must awake to the fact that its future is problematic. American business must take into account the implications of its actions on public opinion, and it must continually explain and justify those actions.

Since much of this explanation and justification is filtered through the media, American business must become successful at manipulating the media if it is to survive.

In this process of explanation and justification, the role of the public relations professional is critical. The public relations executive in particular must have a comprehensive and detailed understanding of the environment of business and how to communicate its message effectively to the public through the news media.

This book is intended to give the reader an understanding of business's environment, particularly as it relates to the media, and to provide a strategy for better business-press relations, with the object being more accurate communication to the public.

Chapter 1 begins with a theoretical overview of the current business climate and the role of the media in shaping it. Subsequent chapters focus on the differences that exist between business and the media and why an adversarial role is likely to exist. The book concludes with several case studies of media management and with practical prescriptions for action.

A NOTE ON THE DATA

Several of the chapters in this book are based on a comprehensive survey of business and the media that I directed for *Business Forum*. Although the data were collected in the latter part of 1982 and compiled in early 1983, the survey remains unique in its comprehensiveness and in its comparison of business executives and journalists. Most of the data derived from the survey have not been duplicated in more recent surveys, and no other survey allows the comparison of the attitudes of journalists, chief executive officers, and public relations executives. Complete documentation and survey results can be obtained by writing: *Business Forum*, School of Business and Economics, California State University, Los Angeles, 5151 State University Drive, Los Angeles, CA 90032.

Information regarding the case studies was collected between December 1985 and June 1986.

I
Theoretical Perspective and Survey Data

1

The New Class and Antibusiness Ideology: A Theoretical Perspective

PRESS HOSTILITY

Business executives often fail to comprehend the hostility of the press toward the business enterprise and its leaders. In part this is because, as New York University Professor Irving Kristol noted in a similar context, most people want to be liked, and when they are not they assume that it is because they are misunderstood. The implicit assumption is: "Understand me better and you'll like me more." The fact that there may be fundamental and irreconcilable differences that divide people is seldom considered. Greater understanding may illuminate rather than shade those differences. An illustration may help.

Although the Soviet Union and the United States have a common interest in avoiding nuclear war, the ideologies of Marxism-Leninism and democratic capitalism are so fundamentally different that they cannot be reconciled. No amount of dialogue aimed at increased understanding can reconcile those differences without change in the tenets of the ideologies. The threat of nuclear destruction may be sufficient to guarantee some sort of mutual accommodation, but given the fundamental differences between the two nations, a genuine mutuality of interests over a comprehensive range of issues simply will not occur.

On a much less global scale, the same fundamental differences exist between a firm and its competitors. In a mature or declining industry, sales increases reaped by one firm mean sales decreases for its competitors. No amount of understanding, dialogue, or even collusion can reconcile this fundamental fact. The OPEC nations attempted to reconcile their differences by establishing a cartel to minimize competition by assigning production quotas. Still, each nation had an incentive to exceed its assigned quota and reap the monopoly profit the cartel made possible. Individual nations could reap monopoly profits only as long as total output did not increase significantly, which in turn was possible only as long as Saudi Arabia—OPEC's largest producer—was willing to compensate for production increases when member nations exceeded their quotas by production decreases of its own. When Saudi Arabia was unable or unwilling to absorb more production increases, total output soared, prices declined, and the irreconcilable differences surfaced.

Irreconcilable differences exist between business and the media. No amount of dialogue and understanding will change that fact. It is even possible that increased understanding and dialogue will highlight these differences and intensify the conflict.

Of course, I do not mean to imply that the differences which divide business and the media are similar in scope and magnitude to the differences which divide Marxism-Leninism and democratic capitalism. In fact, the differences are more like those which divide competitors in a single industry.

To oversimplify, the media are part of what has been called a "new class" of knowledge workers that has emerged with the development of postindustrial society. This new class is in contention with business for the dominant position in society. This competition for dominance forms the basis for the fundamental differences that divide the two groups. Understanding these differences, particularly as they relate to the media, is important because the media helps shape public opinion and influence public policy. Understanding why the media is critical of business will help provide the basis for a more informed and effective media strategy for business.

What follows in this chapter is a theoretical discussion of the development of the new class or intelligentsia in contemporary society and how it relates to the media. For readers not interested in this rather abstract discussion—professors find it difficult to resist theory—it is summarized at the beginning of Chapter 2.

POSTINDUSTRIAL SOCIETY

Harvard professor Daniel Bell first described the characteristics of what he termed "postindustrial" society in a book that was published in 1973.[1] Bell's contention was that the United States was in transition from an industrial to a postindustrial society, and the purpose of the book was to describe the transition and elaborate some of its implications. One of the most important characteristics of postindustrial society, according to Bell, is that it is a high-technology, service-oriented society in which the acquisition and development of formal knowledge plays a critical role. It is not that knowledge was not important to the development of past societies —obviously it was—but that in postindustrial society formal knowledge (as developed and communicated primarily through the system of higher education) is of fundamental importance.

Thus, in postindustrial society the system of higher education – including colleges, universities, research institutes, and the like— becomes a key institution in the society's continued development. The system of higher education is central to development of new knowledge, which is a critical prerequisite to the continued scientific and technological advances that fuel the economy's engine. In addition, the training provided by higher education is critical for performance at the higher levels of the occupational system. A bachelor's or master's, and in some cases a doctoral, degree is required not only for entry-level positions but for long-term career advancement. The rapid expansion of higher education in the past twenty-five years is both a cause and a consequence of the development of postindustrial society.

ACADEMIC LIBERALISM

The structural changes associated with the development of postindustrial society are clear and in the main uncontroversial. The controversial part involves the political and social implications of the changes.

Irving Kristol was among the first to identify what is sometimes referred to as a "new class" of knowledge workers and others that has come about with the advent of postindustrial society. According to Kristol, the new class includes "scientists, teachers and edu-

cational administrators, journalists and others in the communication industries, psychologists, social workers, those lawyers and
doctors who make their careers in the expanding public sector, city
planners, the staff of the larger foundations, the upper levels of the
government bureaucracy, and so on."[2] Although I agree with Kristol's description of the new class, the term is somewhat ambiguous.
An equally or perhaps more appropriate term is "intelligentsia."
The term refers to intellectuals as a political or social group. As will
be argued below, the new class or intelligentsia does have a
collective sense of identity and shares a common political outlook.
For these reasons, the terms "new class" and "intelligentsia" will
be used synonymously. The problem that remains, however, is to
explain how this new class or intelligentsia came into existence.

My contention is that the university is the central institutional
locus of the new class, and the ideology of the new class—including
journalists—is heavily influenced by the dominant ideology of
academics. Many studies have shown that the political ideology of
American academics is further and more consistently left-liberal
than any other identifiable subgroup in the population, including
blacks.[3] Compared to the general public, academics are far more
likely to identify politically as left or liberal, to think of themselves
as Democrats, and to vote for candidates associated with the left-or
liberal wing of the Democratic Party. Compared to the general
public, academics are much more critical of established values and
institutions and much more likely to identify with groups and individuals considered to be similarly critical. Since business is usually
considered the epitome of the establishment, academics tend to
single it out for criticism.

Although not all academics conform to the left-liberal ideological
norm, anyone who has had more than the most casual contact with
the typical professor of, say, history, political science, or sociology
will be struck by the antiestablishment character of his views. Certainly, it is anomalous that these professors, who are highly paid,
high-status professionals, show such animosity toward the institutions and values that accord them their status.

The explanation many academics offer to explain this anomaly is
as follows: academics, devoted to the life of the mind, are accus-
tomed to thinking critically; they are less likely to accept conven-
tional wisdom and more likely to reach beyond the truth of the

moment for a greater and more profound truth. The habit of critical thinking, essential to their intellectual mission, makes them enemies of the status quo. The left-liberal politics of academics is not a "bias" but simply a reflection of their critical intelligence.

However flattering to academics, this explanation does not withstand analysis. Even if it is granted that critical intelligence is a characteristic of academics and that it leads to criticism of existing institutions and values, why are the conclusions so uniformly left-liberal? Academics will sometimes respond that they are taking the values inherent in the American tradition a step further, thus differentiating them from the general public. Undoubtedly, there is some truth to this latter argument. Academics are a type of intellectual and as such have a greater than average commitment to ideas. At the same time academics do not have responsibility for implementing these ideas in the real world. As a consequence, academics in particular and intellectuals in general probably tend to be more "idealistic" than nonacademics or nonintellectuals and less tolerant of societal imperfections.

If this argument is correct, we would expect the politics of academics to be more extreme than that of the general public, which, of course, is the case. We would not, however, expect their politics to be more liberal than that of the public's. The expectation would be that academics would represent the full spectrum of American political opinion in roughly the same proportions but in more extreme form. Academics do not. They adhere to a left-liberal political orthodoxy.

The only explanation consistent with the facts is that academics in certain discipline groupings—primarily the social sciences—are what sociologists call "status incongruent." This means that their status is ambivalent. Everyone's social status is made up of various components or factors. If all of the factors are consistently ranked (high, medium, or low), an individual's status would be congruent. If they are inconsistently ranked (some high, some low), an individual's status would be incongruent. An example of congruent status would be a successful investment banker with an MBA from Harvard, where the high-status business degree is consistent with the high-status job. An example of incongruent status would be an individual with a Harvard MBA employed as a lower-level accountant in a commercial bank. In this instance the high-status degree is inconsistent with the low-status employment. Status incongruence creates difficult social situations—the accountant will constantly have to explain his relative lack of success while the investment banker will not. As a result, people attempt to achieve congruence. In the Fitzgerald novels, the nouveau riche attempt to overcome their common origins (lower status factor) by totally adopting the life-style of the old rich and forsaking their heritage. However, if the lower status factor cannot be changed or denied, there is a tendency to reject the values of the society responsible for its low evaluation. The Harvard MBA working as an accountant will likely devalue the skills and abilities needed for success in commercial banking.

Less obviously, academics in the social sciences face a status incongruence similar to that of the Harvard accountant. As a result of the reliance of postindustrial society on higher education, one aspect of their status, that of being a college professor, is highly evaluated. Another aspect of their status, that of being a sociologist, political scientist, or anthropologist, or such, is evaluated considerably lower. Social scientists simply are not accorded the same authority in their disciplines as are natural scientists. (Note that not all academics are status incongruent. A professor of physics, for example, would not be, since being a physicist and being a college professor are both highly evaluated.)

In frustration over the failure of society to fully accept their expertise, social scientists react against the values and institutions perceived to accord them so little esteem. Academic social scientists thus tend to reject the dominant institutions and values of society, particularly these associated with the traditional "establishment." They reject traditional institutions and values and accept what are identified as "modern" institutions and values because they do not want a return to an industrial or preindustrial society where the role of higher education was much less significant than it is now or likely to be in the future. Thus, these academics identify with what they consider to be the forces of progress and modernity and react against what they consider to be the forces of reaction and tradition.

Since business is associated with traditional values—honesty, hard work, achievement, individual responsibility, and limited government interference—and is considered the epitome of the establishment, it is singled out for criticism. The object is to reduce the power of traditional institutions and values, especially business, and increase the power of academics in particular and the new class or intelligentsia in general. This object is central to the left-liberal political ideology of academic social scientists.

In sum, the status incongruence of academic social scientists encourages them to react against the dominant institutions and values of society and to advocate values and institutions that would enhance their status. In doing this they align themselves with others similarly opposed to the establishment. In concrete terms this results in an ideology critical of the traditional establishment—which explains why academics are antibusiness and so seldom vote Republican—and superficially egalitarian. The rights of "out" groups are championed in the name of equality while the ultimate goal is more power and authority for academics and their allies.

ACADEMICS AND THE NEW CLASS

Although status incongruence can explain the dominant political ideology among academic social scientists, it cannot by itself explain the political ideology of academics as a whole, not to mention that of the new class. This is explained by the existence of a sense of community among academics and the new class, including journalists, that provides a degree of political unity to the two groups.

Within the system of higher education, social scientists—as the "specialists" in social, political, and economic issues—constitute the primary reference group on these matters for the academic community as a whole. The social scientists' perception of political, social, and economic reality is shaped by their left-liberal political ideology. The more closely a person identifies with the academic community, the more likely that person is to subscribe to the social scientists' perception of reality. This explains why academics as a whole, even those in disciplines that are not status incongruent, share the left-liberal political ideology of academic social scientists.

Indeed, the left-liberal political ideology has become associated with academic and intellectual subculture. Many academics like to think of themselves as different from others, and the left-liberal politics of the social scientists allows them to do this. The left-liberal position is identified with an enlightened and progressive way of looking at the world, whereas the conservative view is identified with a narrow defense of special interests and uninformed and perhaps bigoted opinion. Left-liberal politics becomes a sign of membership in an exclusive intellectual community, distinguishing the enlightened from the benighted.

At the center of the new class is the academic community. Closely related to that community is a more inclusive intellectual community. The intellectual community consists of people who work in intellectual occupations concerned with the development of new ideas, such as writers, artists, and scientists, but whose primary employment is not in higher education. Virtually all of these people have college degrees, and many have advanced degrees. These people think of themselves as intellectuals and adhere to the left-liberal political ideology originating within the academic community.

A third, even more inclusive community is composed of knowledge workers. These are people in quasi-intellectual occupations, such as journalists and people in the creative part of the entertainment industry, and in occupations such as public interest law and the higher levels of public administration, such as city planners and health administration officials. Knowledge workers identify with the left-liberal politics of academics either because they identify with intellectuals (as would be the case with journalists) or because their professional interests and that of the new class as a whole are consistent (as would be the case with public administrators).

Figure 1.1 depicts the new class or intelligentsia graphically. Note that the relationship is conceived in concentric circles, with the core being the academic community and the periphery being the knowledge workers. As one moves from the core to the periphery, there is less consistent adherence to the left-liberal orientation. Still, the knowledge workers, while not as extreme as the academics or intellectuals, are disproportionately left-liberal in their politics when compared to the general public. (In Chapter 3, the disproportionate liberalism of journalists is documented.)

Understanding academic politics is important to the subject of this book because academics are influential in shaping opinion and policy in contemporary postindustrial society. Academics exert their influence in two important ways.

The first is by imparting their values on students. Students attend

Figure 1.1
The New Class or Intelligentsia

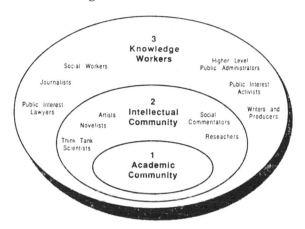

1. The academic community is at the center of the new class or intelligentsia. The strategic importance of academics results from the importance of higher education to the continued development of postindustrial society. The left-liberal political ideology of academics as a whole derives from academic social scientists. The distinctive politics of academics is the basis for mutual identification among the new class or intelligentsia as a whole. Thinking of oneself as an intellectual or identifying with the intellectual community entails adherence to the left-liberal political norm, which in turn distinguishes intellectuals and those who identify with them from others.

2. Intellectuals constitute the second component in the new class or intelligentsia. Included in this group are writers, artists, scientists, and the like not attached direcly to the system of higher education. Individuals in this group tend to think of themselves as intellectuals and share the political views of academics. Their distinctive left-liberal politics is a function of their identification with the intellectual community and serves to distinguish intellectuals from nonintellectuals.

3. Knowledge workers constitute the third element of the new class or intelligentsia. These are people who work in quasi-intellectual occupations, such as journalists and people in the creative part of the entertainment industry, and occupations such as public interest law and higher level public administrators where their interest and that of the new class is similar. Knowledge workers identify with the intellectual community and its politics either because they think of themselves as intellectuals or quasi-intellectuals (as would be the case with journalists) or because their interests and the ideology of the new class is consistent (as would be the case with public administrators).

college to learn, and most of what they learn is factual, uncontroversial, and politically irrelevant. Some of what they learn, however, is politically relevant. Studies have shown that the various disciplines represented in the university are associated with characteristic attitudes and values, including political attitudes and values, and the professors of those disciplines epitomize the norm. Students select disciplines (majors) consistent with their own views and tend to avoid disciplines that are inconsistent. If, for instance, a student is concerned with occupational success, including making a lot of money, the student is more likely to choose business than social work. If a student is politically liberal, he may prefer a major in political science or public administration to one in accounting.

In addition, over time the attitudes and values of students in a particular discipline more closely approximate that of their professors. Students learn the attitudes and values of the discipline from their professors, and the more classes they take, the better they learn the lesson. Thus, the dual processes of self-selection and socialization produce greater and greater conformity of students to the attitudes and values associated with their discipline as they progress through their academic program.

Success in the occupations represented in the new class require a college education, and most often it requires education in the humanities and social sciences, where the left-liberal political ideology predominates. Future journalists, for example, take the preponderance of their courses—at the undergraduate level especially—in the social sciences and humanities. Through the process of self-selection and socialization these students increasingly share the left-liberal political orientation of their professors. After college they enter an occupational milieu consisting of people with similar training, which reinforces their political predispositions.

The second way that academics exert their influence is by virtue of the fact that they are at the center of the broader intellectual community and within broad limits define its political ideology. The collective opinion of academics, particularly the social scientists, as expressed in their publications and lectures, defines the thrust and scope of legitimate intellectual opinion. While few members of the new class actually read the writings of academics or attend their lectures, each probably has a few colleagues who do and who communciate the political essence of the academic message.

To the extent that an individual identifies with the intellectual community, he is likely to assume its distinctive political ideology. The new class in general and journalists in particular tend to identify with this community and assume its left-liberal political ideology. Business and the traditional values with which it is associated are thus seen as the enemies of progress, with progress defined as less influence for business and more influence for the new class and its allies.

CONCLUSION: JOURNALISTS AND THE NEW CLASS

Academics are at the center of the new class or intelligentsia that has emerged with the development of postindustrial society. The politics of academics are predominantly left-liberal and set the ideological tone for the new class as a whole, including journalists.

Taking their cues from the academic community, members of the new class are antiestablishment—they do not recognize that they are often a part of the establishment—and are opposed to traditional institutions and values. In particular, they oppose business and the values associated with it, such as private property, individual responsibility, individual achievement, limited government, the priority of private interests, and so forth. They also tend to identify with the perceived opponents of traditional values and institutions, from socialist governments abroad to excluded minorities at home.

An important occupational characteristic of members of the new class, as Kristol notes, is that they are concentrated in occupations that are in the public or nonprofit sector of the economy. This is true of academics, most other intellectuals, government managers and planners, public interest lawyers, social workers, and so on. By and large it is not true of journalists. Most journalists, in fact, are well-paid employees of very profitable capitalist enterprises. Subjectively, however, journalists do not see themselves as representatives of a private, profit-making company. Rather, they see themselves as representing the public interest and not beholden to any private interest.

Since the early 1960s, with the development of postindustrial society, there has been a rapid growth in the public and nonprofit sector of the economy. Much of this growth has occurred in an attempt to control or circumscribe the private sector. Growth in the size and power of the public sector implies reduction in the size and power of the private sector. Thus, the new class views its institutional interests as being in direct competition with that of business. From both an ideological and institutional perspective, the new class finds itself in an adversarial position with respect to business. Ideologically, business is the most readily identifiable establishment institution. Institutionally, expansion of the power and prerogatives of the new class come with the restriction of the power and prerogatives of business. Thus, the new class finds itself in competition with business for dominance in society. No amount of dialogue or increased understanding between business and the new class will change this fundamental fact.

Before going on to document and elaborate upon these differences, a caveat is in order. In this chapter I have tried to show the objective causes of the left-liberal political ideology of the new class or intelligentsia and why it sees itself in competition with and in opposition to business. This should not imply that members of the new class, whether academic social scientists or journalists, see themselves in a similarly objective fashion. Political beliefs and attitudes are formed and maintained intuitively rather than self-consciously. The reaction against business and the traditional values and institutions with which it is associated is not seen by social scientists as an attempt to overcome status incongruence but as an effort to promote a more enlightened society. The new class does not consciously imitate the politics of academics but identifies with a left-liberal political stance because it seems the more enlightened and progressive. Cues on what opinions are most appropriate and legitimate are taken from respected opinion leaders ranging from Harvard social scientists to the office intellectual.

There is no reason to assume that the new class does not hold its rather distinctive political views in good faith, absolutely convinced —as are business executives—that their views are identical with the interests of society.

NOTES

1. Daniel Bell, *The Coming of Post-Industrial Society: A Venture in Social Forecasting* (New York: Basic Books, 1973).

2. Irving Kristol, *Two Cheers for Capitalism* (New York: Basic Books, 1978), p. 27.

3. See Fred J. Evans, "Toward a Theory of Academic Liberalism," *Journal of Politics*, Vol. 42, No. 4 (November, 1980), pp. 993-1030. This article provides the theoretical and empirical basis for the discussion of academics in this chapter.

2

An Emerging Intellectual Constituency for Business

THE ANTIBUSINESS INFLUENCE

As Chapter 1 showed, the new class or intelligentsia tends to be quite critical of business. This criticism is evidenced in the writings of academics on domestic and foreign policy, the policy prescriptions of think tanks, the bulk of the fictional literature when business is a topic, and from the essays in highbrow intellectual journals to the op-ed pieces and editorials in the local newspaper. In most circles frequented by the new class it is fashionable to be liberal and antibusiness, and any other view must be vigorously defended.

The antibusiness view of the new class is significant because the new class dominates the debate over public policy. To the extent that the debate focuses on businesses' shortcomings, both real and imagined, and minimizes or ignores its strengths, the public is presented with a distorted and negative view of reality. To some extent this is bound to affect public opinion, making it more critical of business than would otherwise be the case.

There are, however, certain developments that have occurred within higher education in the last decade or so that point to a small but significant intellectual constituency for business. If this intellectual constituency were to grow, it would provide a much-needed counterbalance to the business criticism of the new class.

To understand the origins of this intellectual constituency for business, we need to look at changes that have occurred within the academic community.

Although the academic community as a whole is disproportionately liberal and critical of business, there are many very significant internal differences. There are differences by type of school, with academics at the most prestigious institutions being more liberal and critical of business than those at the least prestigious schools. Younger academics tend to be more liberal and critical than older academics. For the present purposes, however, the most important differences are by discipline. From most to least liberal and critical by major discipline grouping are the social sciences, humanities, fine arts, physical sciences, biological sciences, and applied business (i.e., business, engineering, and agriculture). These differences are not minor. The politics of the average professor of sociology will differ vastly from those of the average professor of management.

A survey of faculty opinion illustrates this point very clearly. Asked how they would describe their "overall political inclinations," 63 percent of the social science professors considered themselves far left or liberal while only 23 percent of the business professors responded similarly. In addition, the statement "The private business system in the United States, for all its faults, works better than any other system yet devised for advanced industrial societies" brought agreement from only 62 percent of the social science professors compared to 98 percent of the business professors. Also, most of those in the social sciences who are conservative and neo-conservative more closely identify with society's traditional institutions and values than with academia. Indeed, much of the writing by these scholars is intended to refute the dominant academic view.

ENROLLMENT TRENDS

Within the academic community not only are some institutions more prestigious than others, some disciplines are more prestigious than others as well. The arts and sciences were the founding disciplines of higher education. The professional schools are relatively recent associates and, with the partial exceptions of law and medicine, do not rank as high in prestige as do the arts and sciences.

This is particularly true of business. Even economists sometimes scorn the business school. The attitude of the social scientist is even more disdainful, since anything having to do with making money is not only considered philistine but scarcely worthy of dispassionate scholarly attention.

Until recently students implicitly affirmed this hierarchy, and those with the best academic records chose arts and science majors, leaving the business school with the others. This tendency was dramatized with the baby boom of the late 1950s and 1960s when enrollment in the social sciences increased at unprecedented rates.[1] To illustrate: in 1959-60 the social sciences conferred 51,802 bachelor's degrees compared to 51,522 in business. By 1968-69, however, social science bachelor's degrees had nearly tripled to 155,235 while business bachelor's degrees slightly more than doubled to 106,279.

The result was a dramatic increase in the demand for social science professors. For the typical liberal, intellectually inclined undergraduate, a career in academia appeared very attractive. So the population of the graduate schools swelled with aspiring young academics.

For a time there was an optimistic, indeed, heady atmosphere in the social sciences. Not only were they establishing a more solid scientific claim, but society seemed to be on the verge of admitting how much better off it would be if it heeded the advice of the social scientists. How else could it hope to solve such age-old problems as poverty, racism, and war?

In retrospect, of course, this view seems incredibly naive. Social scientists have not been able to solve these problems, and the demand for social science Ph.D.s has remained almost entirely a function of the demand for teachers. Thus, beginning in the 1970s, when that expansion ceased, job opportunities were reduced radically.

The attractiveness of the social sciences paled considerably with diminishing employment opportunities. Careers in business (and other professions) gained appeal, and business schools across the country gained enrollment. Bachelor's degrees conferred in the social sciences reached a peak of 159,594 in 1971-72. By 1980-81, the most recent year for which figures are available, degrees conferred had declined to 100,647 or nearly 37 percent. During the same period, bachelor's degrees in business increased from 123,306 to 200,876 or nearly 63 percent. This was the first time since 1958-59 that business conferred more bachelor's degrees than social science. Today in the better business schools there are far more applicants than available positions. Many of the best students are considering careers in business.

These enrollment trends have resulted in status changes among academics in the various disciplines. The "impracticality" of the social sciences is mirrored in the relative paucity of students, while the "relevance" of business is mirrored in their relative abundance. The importance of the business professor's position and discipline, as indicated by the number and quality of his students and society's need for them, is quite clear. Rather than academic "poor relations" business professors are now the real "gatekeepers" to the higher-level occupations in the larger society. Both professors and students feel they are participating in the wave of the future and are making a significant contribution to society—a perception remote from the doubt and uncertainty that prevailed in the 1960s.

IMPLICATIONS FOR OPINION FORMATION

As mentioned above, within academia social science professors are the most liberal and critical of business. Because of the relevance of these disciplines to contemporary social problems, they also tend to be the most influential among academics in the formation of political ideology. Indeed, academic social scientists shape the political ideology of the intellectual community as a whole.[2]

This occurs through a process of identification. Being an intellectual is more than just a job; it is a way of life. People who think of themselves as intellectuals assume a characteristic life-style. We might have noticed the professor who wears his hair unfashionably long enough to be fashionable (in intellectual circles) and who maintains studiously careless dress (indicating otherworldly concern). The same is true of attitudes about politics and business. The more closely a person identifies with the intellectual community, the more likely that person will be to consider himself or herself a political liberal and will be more critical of business.

The identification process explains why this diverse group that Kristol calls the new class and Seymour Martin Lipset the intelligentsia is so uniformly critical of business, and the predominance of academic social scientists in defining the political orientation of the intellectual community explains why, almost by definition, business lacks a significant intellectual constituency.

This, of course, does not mean that there are no conservative intellectuals or respected academics who will defend business. In fact, the increasing importance and visibility of neo-conservative and probusiness academics is significant. It does, however, mean that the defenders of business, lacking an institutionalized base, will be scattered throughout the various disciplines and be (and feel) very much in the minority. In this situation their effectiveness as a business constituency is severely limited.

This may not be a permanent condition. Changes are occurring which point to the emergence of an intellectual constituency within the business school. As noted, key to the influence of academic social scientists on the politics of the intellectual is that their professional concerns closely parallel public policy. Thus, one primary reason why business professors have not been influential in the past is because their professional concerns are in many respects irrelevant to public policy considerations—even as they relate to business. The traditional disciplines—accounting, finance, management, or marketing—all relate to some aspect of the firm-customer relationship. In a sense they are all internally focused; broader sociopolitical developments, except as they impinge directly on the day-to-day operation of the firm, are irrelevant. To state the issue differently, the professional concerns of the social science professor pertain to the front or editorial page of the newspaper and those of the business professor to the business page. For instance, as the problems facing our inner cities come to public attention, it is the expertise of the sociologist, political scientist, and economist that is most relevant. Only when a particular proposal is enunciated—say, antiredlining or rent control legislation—does the expertise of the business professor pertain. This helps explain why so few business professors are prominent in the ongoing debate of the future of capitalism. Most of the so-called neo-conservatives come from such unlikely disciplines as philosophy (Irving Kristol), social psychology (Peter Berger), political science (James Q. Wilson), and sociology (Robert Nisbet).

However, the increasing difficulty business has encountered in maintaining a satisfactory relationship with its environment has given rise to an "institutional self-consciousness," an increased awareness that the firm exists and does business in a changing sociopolitical environment and that it must successfully adapt to that environment if it is to continue to exist and do business.

This institutional self-consciousness has given rise to a new discipline in the business school called "business, government, and society," or business and public policy, or business and society. In contrast to the traditional disciplines, this new discipline has an external focus, concentrating on the relation between the firm and the larger society as distinct from customer or potential customer. Thus, the professional focus of academics in this discipline closely parallels public policy concerns. It is relevant in a way that accounting, finance, management, and marketing are not, and it is my argument that academics in this discipline can form the basis of a new intellectual constituency for business.

THE NEW INTELLECTUAL CONSTITUENCY

Although most schools of business offer business and society courses, only a few of the larger ones offer Ph.D.s. Furthermore, there is no systematic data bearing on their politics, and one of the striking things about professors in this field is the diversity of their interests and academic backgrounds. Especially at the larger schools, many have social science rather than business degrees. Why, given this background, are they likely to feel an ideological affinity toward business? There are two important reasons.

The first has to do with recruitment. Academic disciplines have a dominant political orientation: social science disciplines tend to be liberal and antibusiness, while the professional disciplines are conservative and probusiness. Social scientists interested in the "business, government, and society" field are not likely to be, at the very minimum, fanatical socialists. In addition, most business faculty would not want to hire such a professor. Thus, the initial selection process operates to encourage the selection of professors with attitudes roughly consistent with the purposes of the business school.

Also, once an individual becomes a member of a department there are subtle, but nonetheless powerful, constraints toward political conformity. In the typical political science department a conservative probusiness professor is a nonconformist, and it takes a strong personal conviction to maintain such a stance. In the business school the reverse would be true: the liberal antibusiness professor would be the nonconformist. This is not to suggest that there is overt pressure; professors are rarely denied promotion or tenure strictly on the basis of their political beliefs. The process is usually more subtle and inadvertent. Nevertheless, substantial ideological differences do strain collegial relationships.

The second reason is status. Academic social scientists are, in a manner of speaking, professionals without a profession. They enjoy high status as professors but are not accorded commensurate status as social scientists. This is a form of status incongruence which leads to a criticism of the dominant groups and institutions of the larger society.

Professors of business, on the other hand, are not affected by this status incongruence. The business professor has a profession—accounting, finance, management, marketing, or public affairs—and within that profession his status is high because he is a professor. Rather than feeling neglected he feels respected. In changing disciplines, therefore, a social scientist in the business and society field would move from a situation of potential status incongruence to one of status congruence. Once the status of liberalism was removed attitude changes could occur more easily. There are, therefore, very good reasons to believe that the new faculty positions in the business, government, and society field will be filled with academics who, in a fundamental sense, feel comfortable with capitalism and the American business system (though not mindless apologists for it).

If past experience is any guide, as criticism of business increases, the demand for more professors of business, government, and society also will increase, and as the size of such a faculty grows, a sense of competence and strength of purpose will develop. Indeed, these academics could become the catalysts in uniting the more conservative, probusiness faculty in other disciplines –for bringing together, in other words, a coherent intellectual constituency for business. As the field develops, more social scientists can be expected to make contributions on business and society topics to such journals as *Business Forum, California Management Review, Harvard Business Review*, and *Business Horizons*. Similarly, there should be more contributions by business and society professors to such journals as the *Public Interest* and *Commentary*. Thus, a community of scholars will begin to emerge.

This is not to imply that a massive ideological about-face in the intellectual community is imminent. What does seem likely is the emergence of an identifiable group of academics, both respected and respectable in intellectual circles, who unabashedly dissent from the prevailing orthodoxy; who, to paraphrase Michael Novak, do not start with the assumption that capitalistic acts between consenting adults are immoral. It is incumbent upon business to support by helping find research projects, business schools, and research institutes that study business and public policy issues from a less hostile perspective. The result would be a more balanced public debate on capitalism and the American business system.

NOTES

1. For the characteristics of undergraduates by field of study see James A. Davis, *Undergraduate Career Decisions: Correlates of Occupational Choice* (Chicago: Aldine Publishing Co., 1965), Ch. 3.

2. See Daniel Bell, *The Coming of Post-Industrial Society* (New York: Basic Books, 1973), pp. 408-34 passim; Talcott Parsons, "Higher Education as a Theoretical Focus," in *Institutions in Social Exchanges*, ed. Herman Turk and Richard L. Simpson (New York: Bobbs-Merrill Company, 1971), pp. 233-52; A. H. Halsey, "The Changing Functions of Universities in Advanced Industrial Societies," *Harvard Educational Review* 30 (Spring 1960), pp. 118-27.

3

The Politics of the Press:
Liberal and Antibusiness

BUSINESS NEWS IS BIG NEWS

Press coverage of business and economic issues has increased greatly in the last two decades. Within the business community, however, this increased coverage has generated considerable controversy. Business executives frequently believe that much business news coverage is superficial and biased against business.[1] Journalists respond that although business news coverage is not without its flaws, journalists are increasingly well informed and generally do a responsible job in this category of reporting.[2]

In an attempt to assess objectively the adequacy of business and economic news reporting, some analysts have employed the technique of content analysis to the reporting of specific events, such as the Arab oil embargo and nuclear power.[3] The results are mixed. On some issues the coverage appears to be fair or balanced; on others it appears to be biased in one direction or another. This lack of conclusiveness is in part a function of the technique employed. Content analysis tallies frequencies of key words or phrases, experts cited, editorial slant, and so on, to arrive at a quantitative measure of the "balance" of coverage.

Although content analysis can be useful, it says little about why some issues are accorded "balanced" treatment while others are not. To understand why, one must understand something about what motivates the journalist, what his personal views are on business and economic policy issues, what he thinks is newsworthy, what his editors think is newsworthy, and so on. Although imperatives are associated with the particular medium through which news is disseminated—for example, newspapers can provide more detailed coverage of events while television's need to be brief forces simplification—there is evidence that a reporter's basic beliefs, attitudes, and values (his paradigm) will influence how events are perceived.[4] Differences in perception, it seems reasonable to hypothesize, will influence news content. Therefore, understanding journalists' views on basic business and economic issues is likely to help explain the conclusions reached through content analysis.

THE POLITICS OF JOURNALISTS

Reviewing the results of surveys of public attitudes toward business, Lipset and William Schneider note the close correlation between political ideology and political party preference and attitudes toward business. The more one moves from left to right on the political ideology scale, and from strong Democrat to strong Republican on the party preference scale, the more probusiness one is likely to be. Lipset and Schneider conclude, *"Both of these findings confirm the profoundly political nature of the public's attitude toward business"* (emphasis in original).[5]

What is true of the general public is also true of the journalists in our sample. Of the nineteen items in our questionnaire that related to domestic business and economic issues, all but five were correlated significantly with political self-identification or ideology. Party identification (strong Democrat to strong Republican) was correlated significantly with all but nine of the nineteen items. In other words, the more liberal and Democratic the journalist, the more likely he was to be critical of business.

What is the general political orientation of these journalists? Compared to the general public, the answer is overwhelmingly liberal and Democratic. Our survey included the question: "Would you describe your overall political inclination as: far left, very liberal, somewhat liberal, moderate, somewhat conservative, very conservative, far right?" Table 3.1 displays the responses and compares them to those of the general public. In terms of political self-identification or ideology, the journalists place themselves con-

Table 3.1
Political Ideology of Journalists and General Public (percent)

Journalists	Public
50 liberal	22 left
29 moderate	42 center
21 conservative	36 right

siderably to the left of the general population. Fifty percent of the journalists position themselves to the left of center compared to just 24 percent of the public who describe their political inclinations as to the "liberal side." Twenty-one percent of the journalists describe themselves as conservative compared to 38 percent of the public who place themselves on the "conservative side." Twenty-nine percent of the journalists describe themselves as moderate compared to 38 percent of the public who say they are "in between."

Another indicator of political orientation is party preference. We included a question in our survey of journalists that asked: "Do you consider yourself a Democrat, Republican, Independent, or what?" and listed seven alternatives ranging from strong Democrat to strong Republican. Table 3.2 lists the complete breakdown for the journalists and compares them to a Gallup Poll of the general public that included only three alternatives—Democrat, Republican, or Independent. The comparison indicates that the journalists are considerably more likely than the general public to think of themselves as Democrats, considerably less likely to think of themselves as Independents, and about equally likely to think of themselves as Republicans. Although the Gallup and *Business Forum*

Table 3.2
Expressed Party Preference—Journalists and the Public (percent)

	Journalists	Public
Democrat	61	45
Independent	19	29
Republican	20	26

questions were phrased differently, it does appear that the journalists' party preference is more heavily Democratic than the public's preference.

The disproportionate preference of journalists for the Democratic party is reflected in their vote in presidential elections, as Table 3.3 indicates, and the differences are indeed remarkable. In 1972, only 21 percent of the journalists voted for Nixon compared to 62 percent of the public. (The difference of more than 40 percent is the greatest of the three elections. Does this confirm the special animosity that is said to exist between Nixon and the press?) In 1976, 27 percent of the journalists reported voting for Ford compared to 49 percent of the public. In 1980, 25 percent of the journalists voted for Reagan compared to 52 percent of the public. However, not only did the journalists more often vote Democratic and less often vote Republican than the general public, they also were more than three and one-half times as likely to have voted for John Anderson. If, as some have contended, Anderson was the candidate of the new class, it appears that journalists may be a part of that class.

Table 3.3
Presidential Vote, 1972, 1976, 1980—Journalists and the Public (percent)

	Journalists	Public
1972		
Nixon	21	62
McGovern	77	38
1976		
Ford	27	49
Carter	73	51
1980		
Reagan	25	52
Carter	51	42
Anderson	24	7

Note: Figures may not add up to 100 percent due to rounding.

ATTITUDES TOWARD BUSINESS

It is quite clear that compared to the general public, the politics of the journalists in our sample is disproportionately liberal and Democratic, a finding that is consistent with the few other existing studies.[6] The next question is how the politics of journalists relates to their attitudes toward business. Unfortunately, the items on business and economic policy included in the *Business Forum* survey have not been administered in any public opinion polls of which we are aware. The result is that we cannot directly compare the attitudes of journalists and the public on these items. If a direct comparison were possible, we would expect that the comparatively liberal and Democratic journalists would also be comparatively critical of business. We can test this hypothesis indirectly, however, by comparing journalists of different political orientations. What we should find is that the more liberal the journalist, the more likely he is to be critical of business.

Table 3.4 lists the correlations between political self-identification or ideology and attitude on several issues relating to business and economic policy. As mentioned above, of the nineteen items relating to domestic business and economic policy included in the survey, all but five were significantly related to political ideology. The first nine listed in Table 3.4 are those with a gamma of plus or minus .4 or greater. As can be inferred from the gammas for items one and nine in column A, political ideology appears to be related to doubts about the efficacy of capitalism. There is a high correlation ($r = -.736$) between political liberalism and disagreement with the statement, "For all its faults, capitalism or the private market economy works better than any economic system yet devised." Item nine reports a negative correlation ($r = -.406$) between liberalism and agreement with the statement, "Political democracy would be impossible in the absence of free enterprise." Thus, it appears that political ideology is related to estimates about the performance of capitalism as well as its relation to political democracy. The more liberal the respondent, the more likely he is to have doubts on both counts.

Political ideology is related not only to beliefs about the efficacy of capitalism but also to beliefs about the need for regulation. There is a strong correlation ($r = .610$) between liberalism and agreement with the statement "To avoid harm to the public, indus-

Table 3.4
Political Self-Identification and Attitude on
Business and Economic Policy

		A Political I.D. (r)	B Business Influence (r)
1.	For all its faults, capitalism works best.	-.736	N.S.
2.	Regulation is a major cause of productivity decline.	-.629	-.367
3.	To avoid public harm, industry must be regulated.	.610	.500
4.	Reagan's policies will benefit the wealthy and not hurt the poor.	.584	.668
5.	Take big corporations out of private ownership.	.531	.530
6.	Social responsibility requires public scrutiny and oversight.	.517	.326
7.	To compete, U.S. economy needs economic planning.	.485	.344
8.	Wage and price controls are best remedy for chronic inflation.	.470	.444
9.	Political democracy is impossible in absence of free enterprise.	-.406	N.S.
10.	Profits frequently made at expense of average worker.	.337	.611
11.	Political self-identification, liberal to conservative.	--	.569
12.	Social interests and profit interests increasingly divergent.	.385	.434

try must be closely regulated by government." There is also a strong correlation (r = .517) between liberalism and agreement with the statement "The only way to assure that businesses act in a socially responsible fashion is to have vastly increased public scrutiny and oversight of corporate decision making." Thus, political liberalism is related to belief in the necessity for increased government intervention into the economy.

A third pattern relates to the consequences of government intervention in the economy. The more liberal the respondent, the more likely he is to believe that government intervention in the economy will have beneficial consequences. There is, for example, a very strong negative relationship (r = −.629) between liberalism and agreement with the statement "A major cause of the decline of U.S. productivity is excessive government regulation." There is also a strong relationship between liberalism and agreement with the statement "Big corporations should be taken out of private ownership and run in the public interest" (r = .531). Item seven shows the strong correlation between liberalism and agreement with the statement "If the U.S. economy is ever to compete effectively with such economic powers as Japan and West Germany, some form of national economic planning must be developed" (r = .485). There is also a strong relationship between liberalism and agreement with the statement "The best way to halt chronic inflation in the U.S. is by instituting comprehensive wage and price controls" (r = .470). Finally, there is a strong relation between liberalism and agreement with the statement "President Reagan's economic policies will disproportionately benefit wealthy individuals and large corporations and do little to help the poor" (r = .584).

ESTIMATES OF BUSINESS INFLUENCE

Note column B in Table 3.4. This column correlates estimates of business influence with the statements listed in the lefthand column. To determine the respondent's estimate of business influence, we included the following item: "Listed below are several important groups and institutions in American society. On a scale of 1 (a great deal of influence) to 5 (very little influence), rate each according to how much influence they *actually have*." Note that the gammas for the influence item parallel, but are not identical to, those for political ideology. That is, there is a high correlation between political liberalism and the belief that business has a great deal of influence. Item eleven, which correlates the two, yields a gamma of .569. Thus, the more liberal the respondent, the more likely he is to have a high estimate of business's actual influence. Although, as will be shown below, estimates of business influence and political ideology are not identical factors, it does appear that a significant component of the political ideology dimension for journalists is their estimate of the amount of influence or power business has. Comparing the correlations in columns A and B in Table 3.4, it appears that journalists' political liberalism has two components: the belief in the relatively beneficent effects of government intervention and the great actual influence of business which, if unchecked, results in harm to the public. This conjunction gives an ideological basis for an expanded government role in the economy.

Note, however, that political ideology and estimate of business influence are not identical factors. When we correlate the same nineteen variables with influence, while controlling for political ideology, most of the correlations disappear. The two that remain are highly significant, however. There is a partial correlation of .301 between business influence and agreement with the statement "It is frequently the case in this country that the profits of business are made at the expense of the average worker," and a partial correlation of .305 between influence and agreement with the statement "President Reagan's economic policies will disproportionately benefit wealthy individuals and large corporations and do little to help the poor." In both instances we may infer that, independent of political ideology, those individuals who estimate business influence as highest are most likely to believe that that influence is exerted to the detriment of less powerful groups in society.

Note, finally, that not only is there a strong correlation between political ideology and presidential vote but also between vote and estimate of business influence. Table 3.5 summarizes the relationships to presidential vote in the 1972, 1976, and 1980 elections. In each of the elections the relationship is quite strong although somewhat weaker for business influence than for ideology. More important, however, the relationship between business influence and vote obtains when we control for political ideology, with a partial correlation of .280 in the 1972 election, and .271 in the 1976 election. The 1980 vote, in which a substantial number of journalists reported voting for Anderson, is not significant, however.

FACTOR ANALYSIS

Another way of examining the attitudes of journalists toward business is through factor analysis. Table 3.6 lists the loadings on the two principal factors. The first is what may be called a "politi-

Table 3.5

Presidential Vote by Ideology and Business Influence

Vote	Ideology (r)	Influence (r)	Controlling for Ideology (r)
1972	.902	.781	.268
1976	.779	.729	.290
1980	.615	.486	N.S.

Table 3.6

Factor Analysis

"Political" Factor (55.7% of variance)		"Economic" Factor (14.9% of variance)	
1972 Presidential vote	.741	Increasingly, real interests of society and profit interests of business divergent	.657
1976 Presidential vote	.721		
Reagan's policies will benefit wealthy and large corporations, not poor	.702	Frequently profits made at expense of average worker	.648
1980 Presidential vote	.675	Modern marketing techniques promote excessive commercialism	.609
Political ideology	.584		
Business influence	.478	To avoid public harm, industry must be closely regulated	.425
Excessive regulation a major cause of productivity declines	-.401	Profit and loss only concern of most business executives	.418
		Corporate social responsibility requires vastly increased public scrutiny	.408

cal" factor. The variables that load most highly on this factor are presidential vote, attitude toward Reaganomics, political ideology, business influence, and attitude toward regulation. One would expect vote, political ideology, and Reaganomics to load on the same factor. What is surprising is that business influence and regulation as a cause of productivity decline also load on that factor. This association may be explained by remembering that the Democratic Party and liberalism are associated with defense of the disadvantaged and opposition to the advantaged. The more powerful business is perceived to be, the more likely it is to be viewed as advantaged. Similarly, the more powerful business is perceived to be, the less likely regulation will be viewed as hampering its efficiency and causing productivity decline.

The second factor relates more specifically to business and economic policy and may be called on "economic" factor. Items one, two, three, and five relate to the notion that profit does not equal the public interest, items four and six to the notion that the disjunction between profit and the public interest must be resolved through increased government regulation and public scrutiny.

CONCLUSIONS OF THE SURVEY

The sample of journalists in the *Business Forum* survey are much more liberal and Democratic in their politics than the general public. This liberalism is closely related to attitudes toward business: like the public, the more liberal the journalist, the more likely he is to be critical of business. Since journalists are more liberal than the public, we may infer that they are also more critical of business.

Factor analysis suggests that this criticism has two dimensions. The first is distinctly political. Political liberalism and Democratic partisanship traditionally are associated with advocacy of those groups and individuals perceived to be somehow disadvantaged. Advocates of the disadvantaged often believe that progress can be made only at the expense of the advantaged, usually perceived as part of the established order. Business, particularly big business, epitomizes the advantaged establishment. Thus, it is not surprising that attitudes toward business are highly politicized. Neither is it surprising that liberalism is associated with high estimates of business influence, and the more powerful one believes business to be, the less likely one is to believe that government regulation is "excessive" and leads to productivity decline. "Reaganomics," which emphasizes economic growth over redistribution by means of income tax reductions, decreased spending on domestic programs, and reduced business regulation, is a conservative and Republican agenda and engenders more opposition the more liberal the journalist.

The other factor, the "economic" factor, related more specifically to business and economic policy. The items on this factor seemed to relate to the perceived disjunction between the interests of business and the public and the necessity of government regulation to make these interests more consistent. It is obvious that the political and economic factors are closely related. Both assume that business is a significant and advantaged part of the establishment, and both assume that if the interests of the disadvantaged and the public are to be furthered, business power or influence must be curtailed; hence, the criticism of business.

Of course, an explanation of the attitudes of journalists toward business does not prove anything about the content of business news coverage. Journalists may be more critical of business than the general public, and the more liberal the journalist, the more critical he may be; but if, and to what degree, these attitudes are reflected in news copy cannot be tested directly in this study. The study contains one item that indirectly addresses this issue, however. Table 3.7 displays responses to the statement "In general, business news reporting is not critical enough of business." The more liberal the respondent the more likely he is to agree with the statement. Forty-seven percent of the most liberal respondents expressed strong agreement compared to just 7 percent of the more conservative respondents. Only in the strongly disagree column are the responses not significantly different.

We can make some inference about news content from Table 3.7. Although reporters are committed to objective news reporting, how one perceives reality will be determined in part by one's beliefs, attitudes, and values. Any given story about business may be perceived differently depending on one's attitude toward business. If there is a differing perception of stories about business, there are also likely to be differing perceptions about the reality that forms the basis of the stories. The ideal of objectivity will assure that how facts are perceived is how they will be reported.

We would argue that response to Table 3.7 indicates that a process as described above actually does take place. The more liberal the journalist, the more likely he is to think business news reporting is

Table 3.7
Ideology by Business News Not Critical Enough
of Business (row percent)

	Strongly Agree	Agree with Reservations	Disagree with Reservations	Strongly Disagree	N
Far left/ very liberal	47	26	21	5	19
Some liberal	19	50	27	2	54
Moderate	9	52	34	5	44
Some very conservative	7	45	42	7	31

$x^2 = .023$
$r = .309$

not critical enough. The ideal of objectivity encourages more critical stories as one moves along the ideology scale from conservative to liberal, and since journalists as a whole are more liberal than the general public, it is likely that business news in general is proportionately more critical.

Business news reporting is becoming an increasingly specialized function, with more and more reporters assigned full time to a business "beat." Apparently on the theory that familiarity breeds respect, this has led to the belief both within the business community and among journalists that business news reporters are more conservative and less critical of business than general assignment reporters. In our sample, for example, 59 percent of the journalists agreed either strongly or with reservations that "In general, business reporters tend to be more conservative and favorably disposed toward business than the general assignment reporters." Among business reporters, 67 percent expressed agreement compared to 54 percent of the general assignment reporters. Yet when we compare the responses of the two groups on the political and economic items included in the survey, we find few statistically significant differences. However, the differences do vary in the same direction, indicating that business reporters are indeed slightly more conservative and favorably disposed toward business than general assignment reporters. We may tentatively conclude that as business news coverage has expanded it has improved, at least from the point of view of business. However, business reporters remain considerably more liberal and critical of business than the general public, not to mention business executives, and we would expect their stories to reflect this orientation.

Attitudes on business and economic issues are highly politicized among the public and journalists. The more politically liberal the individual, the more likely he is to be critical of business and favor policies that would reduce its autonomy. Journalists, including business reporters, are not a political microcosm of the public but are considerably more liberal and critical of business. To what degree this criticism is reflected in their stories cannot be directly determined by the present study. The indirect evidence strongly suggests a link between ideology and news content: the more liberal the journalist, the more likely he is to believe that present news coverage is not critical enough of business. The inference is that the reporter who values objectivity—who wishes to provide the public with the unvarnished truth—will write stories more critical of business if he believes they presently are not critical enough. The disproportionate liberalism of journalists, including business reporters, supports the contention of many business executives that the press has an antibusiness bias. To paraphrase the title of a recent essay, the evidence indicates that journalists are prodrama and antibusiness.[7]

The findings presented here should give some coherence to the conclusion derived from content analysis by helping to explain why events are reported the way they are. However, to understand precisely how a reporter's paradigm influences his perception of reality and how that is translated into news content, further research is necessary.

APPENDIX: A CASE STUDY IN MEDIA BIAS

In this chapter, evidence was presented showing the liberal, antibusiness bias of the press. Although business reporters were found to be somewhat more conservative and probusiness than general assignment reporters, they were still more liberal and critical of business than the general public.

The liberal, antibusiness ideology of the press would be interesting to academics but not particularly relevant to business were it not for the fact that journalists' ideology influences their perception of reality and therefore how they report the news. Some evidence of this bias was presented in this chapter when it was shown that the more liberal the journalist the more likely he was to believe that current business news reporting was not critical enough of business. It can be inferred from this finding, in the interests of fairness and objectivity, that a journalist so inclined would be more critical of business than current business news reporting. This would be true of both business and general assignment reporters, although the latter would be more critical on average than the former.

An example of how this antibusiness bias manifests itself appears in a book by A. Kent MacDougall entitled *Ninety Seconds to Tell It All*. By his own admission, MacDougall has set out to write the "definitive business-media study." Although he claims allegiance to high standards of "critical analysis and scholarly discipline," the book is something far less than a definitive study, gives no evidence of scholarly discipline, and contains precious little critical analysis.

Such gross inadequacies do not mean that the book is without value. Appearing originally as a series of articles in the *Los Angeles Times*, the book provides insight into and documents the limitations and biases in the news reporter's treatment of business.

Although news reporters in both the print and electronic media have enjoyed increased editorial freedom in the last twenty years, reporters are not yet comfortable with their new, more powerful role and tend to be quite defensive—more defensive, I think, than business leaders, who often are quite timorous. Thus, the news media devotes much energy and attention to prizes and other self-congratulatory displays and little to critical self-analysis. Reporter MacDougall is no exception: he devotes what passes for critical analysis to the minor delicts of the press but concludes with a defense of the basic righteousness of the media. Some examples illustrate.

As can be inferred from the book's title, MacDougall, a career newspaper reporter, is especially critical of the electronic media, particularly television news. Television, unlike newspapers, does not allow enough time to adequately cover most issues. Condensing a complex story into a few seconds of air time oversimplifies and misleads. However, the distortion that occurs is not systematic, says MacDougall, and exhibits no anti-business bias.

In addition, argues MacDougall, there is some chance that news will be distorted—especially broadcast news—by the commercial need to be interesting. Broadcast news depends almost exclusively upon advertisers, and although advertisers do not directly influence the content of the news, the advertising rates charged by the networks are directly related to the broadcast's Nielson rating. Thus, news reporters are forced to compete for their audience and are likely to feature the dramatic and unusual for their entertainment value.

According to MacDougall, however, neither the brevity nor the sensationalism of the electronic media is cause for alarm because there is no intentional, systematic distortion of content, and the print media is available to provide the complete story. The print media (specifically newspapers; news weeklies are not discussed) have all but eliminated sensationalism as a result of the decline of newsstand sales, where dramatic headlines are an important marketing technique. (MacDougall does not explain why news dramatization generates newsstand sales but not subscription sales.)

Thus, according to this "definitive" study, the shortcomings in electronic news reporting are minor deficiencies of that particular medium and are not an indictment of the news media as a whole. Television news, explains MacDougall, is intended only to report news highlights. The citizen who desires to be well informed must assume the responsibility to supplement television news with other news, such as print. (Imagine how MacDougall would react if a manufacturer said that, because of the nature of the medium, advertisements are not very informative and are, in fact, sometimes misleading, but that this is justified because consumers have access to other, more accurate sources of information.)

This example reveals a pattern to MacDougall's arguments: they begin with a discussion of an alleged press shortcoming and conclude with an explanation of why this shortcoming is more apparent than real, unavoidable hence justifiable, or trivial.

Another shortcoming that MacDougall gives some initial credence to is press ignorance: many reporters simply are not qualified to cover complex business and economic news, and their ignorance is reflected in poor reporting. After admitting this possibility, MacDougall immediately goes on to minimize its occurrence. Although occasionally a general assignment reporter will still cover business news, he says, increasingly both the print and electronic media have specialists in business reporting who are informed and who report business and economic news accurately and well. Consequently, MacDougall implies, much of past "reporter-ignorance" criticism of the media is today invalid.

Clearly, the most important issue concerning the adequacy of business news reporting is the political ideology of the press. Do reporters, as many media critics charge, have a liberal, antibusiness bias? MacDougall's answer is an emphatic no. Yet in refuting the charge, he ironically proves the validity of his critics' position.

Consider, in some detail, the chapter entitled "Uncovering Environmental Hazards." MacDougall begins with the obvious and noncontroversial statement that reporters have a responsibility to report environmental hazards, but only on the basis of solid information in order to not alarm workers or the public unnecessarily or cause undue economic harm to industry. However, he then immediately charges that "some companies have reacted defensively to evenly balanced accounts." Even in those few instances where he acknowledges business has been criticized unfairly, it somehow balances out when "the nearly free ride (companies) used to get in the 1950s and 1960s" is remembered. In addition, most of the examples of inaccurate or biased reporting are actually the fault of business for not being open with the press.

MacDougall's own liberal, antibusiness bias is best illustrated by analysis of his discussion of Hooker Chemical Company's role in toxic waste disposal at Love Canal. Initial press reports charged that homes were built on the disposal site and that leaking chemicals caused lesions, miscarriages, birth defects, and other maladies. These charges, many of which Mac-Dougall admits were unfounded, resulted because of Hooker's initial refusal to be open with the press. (The implication is that the press has an obligation to report a story even without access to the facts. If the story proves false, responsibilty lies not with the reporter but with whomever refused to supply the information.)

Subsequently, Hooker did respond to a number of the allegations in the press, noting that: (1) It was not irresponsible in its waste disposal practices given the knowledge that existed from 1942 to 1953 when the dumping occurred, and it should not be judged by contemporary standards; (2) the disposal site was an appropriate one, and the spread of toxic chemicals into the underground water supply was largely a result of negligence by the city; (3) no homes, schools, or playgrounds were built on the toxic waste disposal site; and (4) it had warned the city "the land was unsuitable for construction in which basements, sewers, and other underground facilities would be necessary." The latter fact, which goes a considerable distance toward exonerating Hooker, was published in the *Wall Street Journal* but ignored by most other news sources. This fact MacDougall notes without comment!

One more example is sufficient to illustrate MacDougall's liberal, antibusiness bias. In the course of Occidental Petroleum's abortive takeover bid for the Mead Corporation, a number of internal memos were made public. The memos relating to Hooker Chemical, a subsidiary of Occidental Petroleum, were discussed on CBS's "60 Minutes" in 1979. At issue was the manufacture of the chemical DBCP, which was found to have caused sterility in male production workers. MacDougall recounts a segment of that program:

Reading excerpts from the memo on the air, Mike Wallace came to a sentence in which one plant official suggested to another that the company resume manufacturing DBCP if projected profits comfortably exceeded anticipated legal claims for damaging the health of employees. Wallace read that sentence but not the next one, which specified that resumption of production depended on finding no "significant" risk to Occidental workers.[8]

The reader might then expect MacDougall to illustrate how, through irresponsible and sensational journalism, responsible corporate decisions can be made to appear criminal. The reader would be disappointed. The memos that had been made public, according to MacDougall, "revealed that Occidental and its Hooker subsidiary had followed a pattern in California, Michigan, New York, and Florida of not alerting authorities that their plants were polluting the air and water."[9] The implication? Occidental was guilty of irresponsible if not criminal disregard for the consequences of its actions, both toward its employees and the public. Thus, individual misrepresentations of fact by the press are justified if they illustrate the "real" truth. Imagine MacDougall's indignation if Donald L. Baeder, Hooker's president, advocated such a selective reporting of fact.

The bottom line is that there is a pervasive liberal, antibusiness bias among the nation's press—and this bias affects business reporters no less than general assignment reporters. *Adweek* asked a number of people which newspaper they would like to own and what they would do as owners. MacDougall responded in part as follows:

The *Wall Street Journal*. I'd turn it into a paper that told you how business really operates; how business not only serves the public, but, in serving its own interests, engages in practices that often are not only anti-competition but against the public interest. . . .

I would drag the editorial page, kicking and screaming, into the 20th Century and judge editorial policy, not by whether it promoted business and economic growth, but whether it promoted the quality of life of ordinary American citizens. The *Wall Street Journal* is an excellent paper which, because it can pick and choose what it covers, could be a great paper. But it needs a heart, as well as a head.[10]

That business's and the public's interests ordinarily are not coincident; that economic logic is cold, calculating, impersonal, and often antisocial; and that "human concerns" ought to predominate over the crass commercialism of capitalism are views held by MacDougall and shared by the vast majority of his colleagues. Even publications devoted exclusively to business news reporting reveal a liberal, antibusiness bias, as Steven Largerfield demonstrated of *Business Week*.

In an important article, "The Media and Business Elites" appearing in *Public Opinion*, S. Robert Lichter and Stanley Rothman help explain the origins of press bias. The politics of the "media elite," Lichter and

Rothman demonstrate, is predominately liberal, as indicated by their political self-identification (54 percent left of center), voting record (overwhelmingly Democratic), and attitudes on social issues (favor redistribution for the disadvantaged, quality-of-life orientation).

The attitudes of the media toward the economy and business that this study reveals are particularly interesting. On the one hand, the media elite support capitalism: they do not favor nationalization of large companies; they favor less regulation of business and support differential economic reward based on merit. On the other hand, they remain profoundly critical of business because they believe that business leaders have more power than they deserve. Media elites believe that business is the most influential group in society but that the media ought to be. Thus, media criticism of business appears to be based on their belief that business is the major leadership group with whom they are in contention for power. To an unknown degree this bias affects public opinion and is translated into public policy.

Efforts to correct press bias will be futile as long as reporters persist in their ideological complacency. Unlike their European colleagues, American journalists generally value political neutrality or "objectivity," and most reporters believe that their primary responsibility is to report the "facts." Although recognizing the possibility of ideological distortion in others, they deny it in themselves. Stephen Hess, in *The Washington Reporters*, asked a sample of Washington-based journalists if they thought there was any press bias. A majority responded yes, and of those respondents almost all said the bias was left or liberal. When Hess asked them about their own politics, most said they were moderate or middle-of-the-road. Lichter and Rothman also found that members of the press tend to judge their colleagues as more liberal. This reveals not, as Hess concluded, that reporters are in fact middle-of-the-road or that they misperceive the politics of their colleagues, but that individually they feel they are politically neutral or unbiased.

This view leads to astounding ideological complacency, as revealed unwittingly by MacDougall. Although an excellent case can be made that an important affliction of Americans in general and American business in particular is a lack of self-confidence, the opposite must be said of the American news media.

Much news reporting is entirely inadequate and misleading and reflects the liberal, antibusiness ideology of reporters—to the detriment of the public and public policy. This shortcoming will not be corrected until those who create the news undertake serious self-criticism.

NOTES

1. This is particularly true of television news reporting. Newspapers are rated more favorably, but negative responses far outnumber positive

responses even in this medium. See the *Business Week*/Harris Poll, "Business Thinks TV Distorts Its Image," *Business Week* (October 12, 1982), p. 26. The *Business Forum* study results also confirm this negative image.

2. A recent defense of business news reporting is by *Los Angeles Times* reporter A. Kent MacDougall, *Ninety Seconds to Tell It All* (Homewood, Ill.: Dow Jones-Irwin, 1981).

3. Recently, a number of studies utilizing this approach have been conducted under the auspices of the Media Institute, a business-oriented research organization.

4. The origin of the term "paradigm" to explain how individuals perceive reality differently is from a book by Thomas Kuhn, *The Structure of Scientific Revolutions* (Chicago: University of Chicago Press, 1962). For a recent attempt to explain the paradigm of journalists see Stanley Rothman, "The Mass Media in Post-Industrial Society," in *The Third Century: America as a Post-Industrial Society*, ed. Seymour Martin Lipset (Stanford, Cal.: Hoover Institution Press, 1979), pp. 361-76. For evidence that a journalist's paradigm will influence his perception of reality see Stanley Rothman and S. Robert Lichter, "Media and Business Elites: Two Classes in Conflict?" *The Public Interest* (Fall, 1982), pp. 121-25.

5. Seymour Martin Lipset and William Schneider, "How's Business? What the Public Thinks," *Public Opinion* (July-August, 1978), p. 47.

6. John W. C. Johnstone et al., *The News People* (Chicago: University of Illinois Press, 1976), pp. 92-93; Stephen Hess, *The Washington Reporters* (Washington, D.C.: The Brookings Institution, 1981), p. 115; and S. Robert Lichter and Stanley Rothman, "Media and Business Elites," *Public Opinion* (October-November, 1961), pp. 42-46, 59-60.

7. J. Herbert Altschull, "Journalists Aren't Anti-Business—They're Just Pro-Drama," *Business Horizons* (September-October, 1982), pp. 7-6.

8. MacDougall, *Ninety Seconds*, p. 88.

9. Ibid., p. 89.

10. "Special Report: Newspapers Fight Back!" *Adweek* 31, no. 18 (April 27, 1981), p. nr84.

4

Business and the Media: Contentious Contenders

THE BUSINESS-MEDIA CONTROVERSY

A great deal of concern has been expressed recently about relations between business and the media, at least among business executives and journalists. This concern reveals a controversy between business executives and journalists about the quality and fairness of business-news coverage. This controversy has escalated in the last 10 to 15 years, as business news began receiving greater prominence in the media. Traditionally, business news consisted mostly of reporting on financial markets, new product entries, executives recently hired or promoted, and the like. The news was not ordinarily controversial, much of it having been compiled from business press releases. In newspapers, business news usually appeared somewhere behind the sports section, where only its limited business audience would find it.

Business news became of general public significance beginning in the late 1960s and early 1970s. Such newly emergent issues as equal opportunity, consumerism, and environmentalism brought business to the front page but often in a way that made it appear to be a major obstacle to progress. Add to this the seemingly endless economic problems of the 1970s—skyrocketing oil prices, recession, unemployment, inflation—and business news coverage seemed to many business executives as hostile, indeed. Faced with such accusations from business, reporters, for the most part, responded that they were not hostile toward business but simply reporting events as they occurred. If a controversy exists, they said, reporters cannot ignore it.

All of this resulted in an outpouring of writing on the subject by assorted business executives, journalists, and academics.[1] Much of this literature—some of it adapted from symposia and group encounter sessions designed to get business executives and journalists engaged in dialogue—was in the genre of "understand me better and you'll love me more or at least hate me less." Whether better business-media relations resulted, we do not know.

What we do know is that, other than the opinions expressed by a few selected journalists and business executives, little of an empirical nature has been done to assess and compare the attitudes of journalists and business executives on media coverage of business.[2] This chapter systematically examines the attitudes of journalists and business executives on the role of the press in society and the adequacy of business news coverage. Analysis of the attitudes of the two groups—particularly the differences between them—provides considerable insight into the controversy between business and the media. It also provides a solid basis for recommendations on how to improve business-media relations.

THE MEDIUM IS THE MESSAGE

Marshall McLuhan first popularized the idea that the medium of communication influences the content of the message. Although few today would go as far as McLuhan on the importance of the medium, it would be incorrect to deny that it has some—at times very significant—effect on the content of the message. A *Business Week*/Harris Poll hints that one cause of the low rating business executives give television news is the perceived necessity of that medium to be entertaining.[3] The survey not only confirms and elaborates on this concern of business but also shows that journalists and business executives hold very different views on the effects of entertainment on news content.

The vast majority of both journalists and business executives agree that "most" reporters will choose the dramatic and unusual story over the commonplace and mundane." Indeed, a journalist in this study volunteered that "almost by definition, 'news' is something other than a recapitulation of the commonplace and mundane." Most of our respondents would probably agree. Note, however, the response differences in the "strongly agree" category of Table 4.1. Only 32 percent of the journalists strongly agree with the statement compared to 70 percent of the public affairs executives (PAEs) and 76 percent of the chief executive officers (CEOs).[4] This difference reflects the belief of business executives that journalists give priority to entertainment to the detriment of content. Journalists, of course, disagree.

Consider responses to the following: "An attempt to make news entertaining seriously distorts its content." Only 24 percent of the journalists agreed with the statement compared to 76 percent of the PAEs and 77 percent of the CEOs. Journalists acknowledge the need to be entertaining but deny that it results in significant news distortion. Business executives are convinced that the medium is the message—that the attempt to entertain seriously distorts news content. Therefore, it should not be surprising to find that business executives also are much more likely than journalists to agree that "competition for readers results in lower quality news." Only 21 percent of the journalists agree with the statement compared to 63 percent of the PAEs and 79 percent of the CEOs.

The quite different perceptions of journalists and business executives regarding the effects of entertainment on news content can be examined from another perspective. For both journalists and business executives there is a positive correlation between the belief that the "attempt to make news entertaining seriously distorts its content" and that "competition for readers results in lower quality news." Note, however, that the correlation is significantly stronger for business executives than journalists and that a much higher proportion of business executives than journalists is likely to agree with each of the statements. The implication is that the issues of entertainment and news distortion are of considerably less importance to journalists than to business executives.

This view is confirmed by the positive correlation for business executives between the belief that "reporters will choose the dramatic and unusual story" and "entertainment distorts news content" and "competition lowers news quality" and by the absence of a significant correlation between these three variables for journalists. Business executives, in other words, seem convinced that journalists must entertain to attract an audience and that the need

Table 4.1
Entertainment and News Distortion

		Strongly Agree	Agree with Reservations	Disagree with Reservations	Strongly Disagree
There is an element of entertainment to news reporting, and most reporters will choose the dramatic and unusual story over the commonplace and mundane.	Journalists	32	54	11	4
	PAEs	70	25	5	–
	CEOs	76	22	2	–
An attempt to make news entertaining seriously distorts its content.	Journalists	7	18	55	21
	PAEs	25	51	22	2
	CEOs	26	51	22	2
In journalism, competition for readers tends to result in lower quality news.	Journalists	8	13	38	42
	PAEs	24	38	28	10
	CEOs	36	43	17	5

Note: Figures may not add up to 100 percent due to rounding.

to entertain is the source of much news distortion. Journalists acknowledge the need to entertain but deny that it has any significant distorting effect.

A statistical procedure called "discriminant analysis" provides another perspective on the differences between journalists and business executives. This analysis enables a statistical distinction to be made between two or more groups on the basis of a given number of distinguishing features or independent variables. Comparing journalists and CEOs, the three variables correctly predict group membership in 80 percent of the cases for CEOs and in 77 percent of the cases for journalists and PAEs. These relatively high percentages (50 percent would indicate a chance relationship) are indicative of the substantial differences that exist between the two groups. The three variables do not contribute equally to the distinction, however. "Competition results in lower quality news" distinquishes journalists and business executives most, followed by "entertainment distorts" and then by "reporters will choose the dramatic and unusual story." Thus, journalists and business executives disagree most on the effect of entertainment on news content.

THE PROFESSIONAL IMPERATIVE

The press in the United States enjoys a constitutionally protected independence seldom equaled even in other modern liberal democracies. Equally unique is the tradition of objectivity that it enjoys. In Europe, the press frequently was an instrument of a particular party—both political and religious—and events were interpreted to advance the party's position. In the United States, especially after the middle of the nineteenth century, formal press partisanship declined, and reporters tended to see their role as simply reporting the "facts." Thus, the press in the United States had a history of greater freedom and independence and a stronger commitment to "objectivity" than the press in most European countries.[5]

In the last several decades, however, the independence of the journalist has increased significantly. Formerly, "the reigns of authority were in the hands of the publishers, and reporters who wanted their jobs stayed in line. Publishers . . . also actively catered to the preferences of their advertisers."[6] In business reporting, for example, journalists were frequently "two hatters," both writing business news and selling advertising. Increasingly, the editorial side of the newspaper has been separated—indeed, insulated—from the business side, and reporters enjoy much more autonomy than before. All of this gives increased prominence to the individual reporter and raises the following questions: What should the role of the reporter be in presenting the news? Should the reporter attempt to report only the "facts" or should he offer some interpretation? Should the reporter actively encourage the development of "better" public policy? Since the reporter works in a commercial enterprise, what should his relationship be to his publisher? How much, if any, influence should publisher and advertiser exert over news content? Our survey allows us to answer these and similar questions.

Responses to the survey indicate that journalists tend to see themselves as keepers of the public trust and consider exposing violations of it as an important component of their job (see Table 4.2). Ninety-six percent of the journalists agreed that they "have a moral and professional obligation to act as public watchdogs and publicize violations of the public trust even though those violations may not be illegal." A smaller, though still substantial, number of PAEs (81 percent) and CEOs (72 percent) also agreed with this role of the journalist. The differences between journalists and business executives are more pronounced when we look at the "strongly agree" responses: nearly two-thirds of the journalists strongly agree with the statement compared to just one-fifty of the PAEs and one-tenth of the CEOs. Thus, journalists strongly identify with the public watchdog role and see their mission as exposing readers to violations of the public trust. While a substantial majority of business executives concur in this view of the press, they do so less strongly. This, I suspect, is because of the subjective character of a "violation of the public trust." Journalists and business executives disagree strongly on many substantive issues, and what a journalist may perceive as a trust violation may not appear as such to the business executive.

This hypothesis is supported by responses to the statement that the "personal political and economic views (of reporters) inevitably will influence the content of their stories." Sixty-three percent of the reporters agree with the statement compared to 90 percent of the PAEs and 94 percent of the CEOs. However, responses in the

Table 4.2
Professional Standards

	Strongly Agree	Agree with Reservations	Disagree with Reservations	Strongly Disagree
Journalists have a moral and professional obligation to act as public watchdogs, and should seek out and publicize violations of the public trust by leaders of major institutions, even though those violations may not be illegal.				
Journalists	64	32	3	1
PAEs	20	61	14	5
CEOs	11	62	21	6
Regardless of how objective reporters try to be, their personal political and economic views will inevitably influence the content of their stories.				
Journalists	17	46	30	7
PAEs	50	40	9	1
CEOs	61	33	5	1
A reporter plays an important educational role not only in reporting events to the public but also in pointing out their significance.				
Journalists	78	20	3	1
PAEs	47	39	10	5
CEOs	34	43	17	6
An important component of the reporter's job is to encourage the development of better public policy.				
Journalists	23	42	24	11
PAEs	14	32	30	24
CECs	16	33	31	21

Note: Figures may not add up to 100 percent due to rounding.

"strongly agree" category reveal the greatest divergence of opinion: only 17 percent of the reporters strongly agree compared to 50 percent of the PAEs and 61 percent of the CEOs. Reporters tend to see themselves as objective and unbiased; after all, the legitimacy of their role as public watchdogs depends upon their objectivity. Business executives, observing the same issues from a perspective quite different from the journalist, are more sensitive to what they perceive as press bias.

Disagreement regarding the advocacy role of the press also exists. Two items on this issue were included. One was a relatively neutral statement: "A reporter plays an important educational role not only in reporting events to the public but also in pointing out their significance." Ninety-six percent of the journalists agreed as did 87 percent of the PAEs and 77 percent of the CEOs. Note that although there is strong agreement expressed by all respondent groups, journalists give almost unanimous assent. Note also that the statement avoids the implication of advocacy—pointing out the significance of an event does not necessarily imply advocating a policy or course of action. A second item included in the survey is less neutral: "An important component of a reporter's job is to encourage the development of better public policy." Sixty-five percent of the journalists agreed with this statement compared to 56 percent of the PAEs and 49 percent of the CEOs. For all three groups there is a significant decline in agreement. Thus, while there is considerable support for a relatively neutral educational role for the press, there is much less support for what may be perceived as press advocacy. The ideal of press objectivity or neutrality seems to remain influential.

Discriminant analysis again aids in evaluating the differences between journalists and business executives. Comparing journalists and CEOs, three variables ("encourage the development of better public policy" was not significant and therefore excluded from the analysis) correctly predict group membership in 82 percent of the cases. Comparing journalists and PAEs, the four variables correctly predict group membership in 75 percent of the cases. While these variables significantly distinguish journalists from business executives, in both instances responses to the statement that journalists should encourage the development of better public policy contribute least. This tends to confirm the belief that there is a relatively high degree of consensus in favor of neutral or objective reporting.

JOURNALISTIC AUTONOMY

The next issue relates to how much editorial control publishers and advertisers can and should have over news content (see Table 4.3). One of the few responses that did not significantly distinguish journalists from business executives related to the right of business to withhold advertising when it feels it has been unfairly criticized. Eighty-eight percent of the journalists agreed that business has this right compared to 86 percent of the PAEs and 92 percent of the CEOs. However, a hypothetical right does not necessarily imply wise practice. The view of business may have been summarized by a CEO who volunteered "because a right exists does not mean it should be exercised." The surprising finding was the extent to which reporters agreed to this "right." In general, as will be shown below, reporters do not see the commercial context in which they function as a threat to their professional integrity any more than they perceive the need to be entertaining as a significant cause of news distortion.

There was little agreement among journalists and business executives that paid advertising threatens objective news reporting. Seventy-eight percent of the journalists disagreed, as did 83 percent of the PAEs and 82 percent of the CEOs. Although there is less concern among business executives than journalists about the threat of advertising to objective news reporting, the rather remarkable finding is how little concern reporters seem to have. This finding, combined with the attitudes of reporters on the need to be entertaining, indicates that they are rather well adapted to the commercial constraints of private journalism.

If advertisers do not have significant control over news content, what of publishers? We included two items concerning this issue. One item related to specific stories: "Editors and publishers should 'kill' or tone down a story that is excessively critical of important groups or individuals." Eighty-two percent of the journalists disagreed with the statement compared to 75 percent of the PAEs and 67 percent of the CEOs. Although disagreement is substantial for all three groups, it is highest for journalists—whose stories might be killed—and lowest for CEOs—who constitute "important individuals."

Another item related to the more general role of the publisher is controlling content of the news. The statement read, "As owners, it

Table 4.3
Journalistic Autonomy

	Strongly Agree	Agree with Reservations	Disagree with Reservations	Strongly Disagree
Business has a right to withhold advertising when it feels it has been unfairly criticized in the press.				
Journalists	63	25	6	6
PAEs	61	25	8	7
CEOs	73	19	6	2
Paid advertising threatens objective news reporting because stories critical of advertisers may result in a loss of revenue.				
Journalists	7	15	33	45
PAEs	3	13	37	47
CEOs	1	18	45	36
Editors and publishers should "kill" or tone down a story that is excessively critical of important groups or individuals.				
Journalists	3	15	27	55
PAEs	6	20	42	32
CEOs	8	26	43	23
As owners, it is legitimate for publishers to set the overall editorial tone and news content of the stories produced by journalists who work for them.				
Journalists	14	28	24	35
PAEs	22	38	25	11
CEOs	23	55	14	8

Note: Figures may not add up to 100 percent due to rounding.

is legitimate for publishers to set the overall editorial tone and news content of stories produced by journalists who work for them." In essence, the statement says that the owners have a right to control the type and quality of the product produced by their company. In any business but the media, this right would seem self-evident. Indicating the extent to which journalists consider their case exceptional, 58 percent disagreed. This contrasts sharply with the 40 percent disagreement among the PAEs and 22 percent among the CEOs. Clearly, the journalists feel that they are entitled to a high degree of editorial autonomy—a view not as widely held by business executives.

It is interesting that among the journalists there is a relatively weak but statistically significant relationship between "publishers should set editorial tone" and "personal views of reporters will influence news content" (r = .1716). Thus, the more likely a journalist is to believe the news is objective or neutral, the less likely he is to believe that it is appropriate for editors or publishers to try to influence the editorial content of his stories. To the reporter who strongly believes in his objectivity, such interference could only appear arbitrary.

Discriminant analysis shows that, for the variables discussed in this section, there is much less disagreement between journalists and business executives than was the case for the variables discussed in the previous sections. Comparing journalists and PAEs, the variables correctly classify the journalists and PAEs in 61 percent of the cases. For the CEOs the percentage is 68. In both comparisons the two variables that contribute most to the distinction are "editors should kill excessively critical stories" and "it is legitimate for publishers to set overall editorial tone." This reconfirms the conclusion drawn above: journalists are relatively satisfied with the commercial context of their profession and do not view advertising as a serious threat to their independence. Journalists, however, tend to be sensitive about encroachments by editors and publishers on their professional autonomy.

EDITORIAL CONTENT: TWO VIEWS

A concern expressed by many business executives is that reporters are excessively critical of business and that this attitude is reflected in their reporting. Journalists deny that they are especially critical of business or that this criticism is reflected in their stories. This section examines the attitudes of journalists and business executives on business news reporting.

An item that most strongly distinguished journalists from business executives read, "In general, business news reporting is not critical enough of business" (see Table 4.4). Sixty-four percent of the journalists agreed with the statement compared to just 12 percent of the PAEs and 7 percent of the CEOs. An extrapolation of this result would be that nearly two-thirds of the journalists believe that fairer press coverage of business would require more criticism, whereas nine-tenths of the business executives believe that fairer coverage would require less criticism! This statement taps the source of much conflict between business and the media: journalists believe that they are doing a creditable job and perhaps being more than fair to business; business executives feel victimized by a generally hostile press.

This view is confirmed by comparing responses to the statement "Political and economic views of reporters will influence the content of their stories" with the statement "business news is not critical enough." Attitude toward these items is not significantly related for the journalists but is for the business executives. Thus, the more likely business executives are to believe that journalists' stories reflect their personal views, the more likely they are to also think that business news is too critical. In other words, the view that reporters are biased against business and that this is evident in their news coverage holds some currency among business executives. The lack of correlation among the journalists indicates that they hold no such view.

Importantly, however, both business executives and journalists distinguish between business and general assignment reporters. Fifty-nine percent of the journalists, 69 percent of the PAEs, and 71 percent of the CEOs agreed that "business news reporters tend to be more conservative and favorably disposed toward business than general assignment reporters." Also interesting to note is that, by a margin of 67 percent to 54 percent, business reporters are more likely than general assignment reporters to agree with this statement. Business reporters apparently feel more conservative and probusiness than their colleagues.

Table 4.4
Editorial Content: Two Views

		Strongly Agree	Agree with Reservations	Disagree with Reservations	Strongly Disagree
In general, business news reporting is not critical enough of business.	Journalists	17	47	32	4
	PAEs	3	9	52	35
	CEOs	1	6	40	53
In general, business reporters tend to be more conservative and favorably disposed toward business than general assignment reporters.	Journalists	9	49	32	9
	PAEs	12	57	23	9
	CEOs	12	59	24	6
In general, business reporters tend to be more conservative and favorably disposed toward business than general assignment reporters.	Gen. Assign.	7	47	38	7
	Business Reporter	14	53	23	11
In general, business news reporting is not critical enough of business.	Gen. Assign.	21	48	28	3
	Business Reporter	12	44	41	4

Note: Figures may not add up to 100 percent due to rounding.

If business reporters are indeed more favorably disposed toward business than general assignment reporters, we would expect them to be less likely to agree that business news reporting is not critical enough. This is the case. Fifty-six percent of the business reporters compared to 69 percent of the general assignment reporters agree that business news is not critical enough. However, there may be some defensiveness on the part of business reporters. When we compare the responses of business reporters with general assignment reporters on various business and economic policy issues and political attitude items, we find that the actual differences are quite small. On most of these items business reporters do tend to be more conservative and probusiness than their colleagues, but in most cases the differences are too small to be statistically significant.

The reason the differences are relatively minor probably has to do with the recruitment process in journalism and the fact that journalists are part of the new class. Journalists typically are trained as generalists rather than experts. Business reporters are no more likely than general assignment reporters to have degrees in business. Reporters typically are assigned a beat rather than preparing for one. In a telephone interview, the business editor of a West Coast newspaper said it was his experience that "most reporters do not want a business assignment, and rather than asking for it they are assigned to it." The editor of the business section of a large Midwest newspaper confirmed this view, noting that most reporters assigned to him had no formal training in business and that although he had an MBA, he took it after he had become a business reporter.

Thus, reporters—including business reporters—typically are trained in the more liberal, antibusiness disciplines—English, the social sciences, journalism—and bring those views to their professional endeavor. These views, in turn, are reinforced by their colleagues. That business reporters become somewhat more conservative and probusiness than their colleagues is probably because they begin to identify with their subject matter. As knowledge workers, however, they also identify with the liberal, antibusiness politics associated with the new class or intelligentsia.

IMPROVING BUSINESS REPORTING

Business executives are quite unhappy with the quality of business and economic news, and while few journalists are equally dissatisfied, I suspect that few would deny the possibility of improvement. On the question of what can be done to improve the quality of business journalism, however, there is much disagreement between business and the press (see Table 4.5).

We have already seen that there is great disagreement about the quality of business journalism and whether it is too critical of business, but there is a more fundamental disagreement about the appropriate qualifications of journalists. With a few exceptions, journalists tend to see themselves as generalists. We included the statement "To be a good reporter, one need not be an expert on the subject reported on." Eighty-eight percent of the reporters agreed compared to 64 percent of the PAEs and 59 percent of the CEOs. Even more revealing is the "strongly agree" responses, with nearly one-third of the reporters agreeing strongly compared to just one-eighth of the business executives.

Although reporters in general see less need for substantive expertise than CEOs, this does not translate into the view that substantive knowledge is irrelevant. A nearly unanimous 96 percent of the reporters agreed that "Business news reporting could be substantially improved if reporters had more knowledge about business and economic affairs." This compares to a nearly identical 96 percent agreement for the PAEs and 95 percent agreement for the CEOs. Again, however, the significant divergence occurs in the "strongly agree" category where 40 percent of the journalists fall compared to 82 percent of the PAEs and 77 percent of the CEOs. Also interesting to note is that for journalists there is no significant relationship between the belief that "a good reporter need not be an expert" and "more knowledge would improve business news reporting." Reporters apparently believe that substantive knowledge is not necessary for good reporting but that additional knowledge helps. For the business executives, however, there is a negative relation between the two. Thus, business executives appear to place greater emphasis on the importance of substantive knowledge, whereas journalists may place greater reliance on ability to recognize a good story.

Discriminant analysis sheds further light on the differences between business and the press. Four of the variables discussed in this section—"business reporting is not critical enough," "the personal views of reporters will influence the content of their stories," "good reporters need not be experts," and "more knowledge

Table 4.5
Improving Business Reporting

	Strongly Agree	Agree with Reservations	Disagree with Reservations	Strongly Disagree
To a good reporter, one need not be an expert on the subject reported on.				
Journalists	32	55	12	1
PAEs	15	53	21	12
CEOs	10	50	31	10
Business news reporting could be substantially improved if reporters had more knowledge about business and economic affairs.				
Journalists	49	45	5	1
PAEs	82	15	3	1
CEOs	77	18	3	2

Note: Figures may not add up to 100 percent due to rounding.

would improve business reporting"—correctly distinguish journalists from CEOs in 86 percent of the cases. The variable that contributes most to the distinction is "business news is not critical enough" (see also Table 4.4). Journalists and business executives could hardly be farther apart on the matter; the item seems to epitomize the contention between business and the press. The variable that next most powerfully distinguishes the two relates to the objectivity of reporters. Reporters are much more likely than business executives to think that news reporting is "objective" and uninfluenced by their personal views. This is a view simply not shared by most business executives. Business executives typically feel that journalists are biased against business and that this shows in their stories. The final two variables that distinguish journalists from business executives relate to how much substantive knowledge is necessary for good reporting. In both cases—"reporters need not be experts" and "more knowledge would improve business news" —business executives are more likely than reporters to believe substantive knowledge is necessary.

Thus, compared to business executives, journalists are more likely to believe that general knowledge is sufficient for good reporting, that their personal views do not influence the content of their stories, and that business news is fair or even less critical than is warranted.

SUMMARY AND CONCLUSIONS

Journalists and business executives differ rather dramatically on many issues relating to the role of the press on society and the adequacy of business news coverage.

The journalists are relatively well adapted to the commercial context within which they work. While they think business has a right to withhold advertising when it feels unfairly criticized, journalists do not feel threatened by editorial pressure from advertisers. Although the journalists are for the most part employees of private corporations, they do not see themselves as under the direct control of "management." Fifty-seven percent disagreed that it is legitimate for publishers "to set the overall editorial tone and news content of stories produced by journalists who work for them." The apparent concern of journalists is that objective news reporting would be impaired by arbitrary intervention of publishers and editors. Not only are business executives more likely to agree that it is legitimate for editors and publishers to set the editorial tone, but they are less likely to consider the result an infringement on press objectivity.

Journalists typically are not substantive experts; political reporters do not necessarily have degrees in political science, police reporters in criminology, or business reporters in business; and although journalists believe that more knowledge is better than less, they do not believe that a great deal of substantive knowledge is necessary for good reporting. Business executives strongly disagree on this point, echoing the often-stated complaint that reporters simply do not know enough about business to report it adequately.

Another area of strong disagreement relates to the distorting effects of entertainment. Both journalists and business executives recognize that journalists must be entertaining to attract and hold an audience. The point of contention is that journalists do not believe that entertainment results in news distortion, whereas business executives believe strongly to the contrary.

Journalists closely identify with the role of public watchdogs and consider it their obligation to find and report violations of the public trust. More than three-fourths of the business executives agree with this press role but do so less strongly than journalists, perhaps because of the subjective character of a trust violation. The ideal of press neutrality or objectivity seems to hold some currency for both groups. A high proportion of both journalists and business executives believes that it is appropriate for journalists to point out the significance of an event, but agreement drops off considerably when the propriety of journalistic advocacy is addressed.

Journalists are much more likely than business executives to believe that their reporting is unaffected by their personal views. Business executives are much more likely than journalists to believe that reporters are biased against business and that this shows in their stories. Both journalists and business executives believe that business reporters are more conservative and favorably disposed toward business than general assignment reporters, and although there is some truth to this view, the differences are not as great as might be expected.

If there is a single theme that runs through all of the issues discussed in this chapter, it is that journalists believe they are doing an acceptable job of objectively conveying needed information to the public. In fact, with respect to business news, if journalists feel they err, it is because they treat business too favorably.

For anyone who has had some personal contact with journalists, the view that the reporter is somehow above the battle, detached from the play of special interests on which he dutifully reports to the public, will strike a familiar chord. As we have seen, journalists strongly identify with the public watchdog role, and, indeed, their situation is similar to that of the various "public interest" groups and unlike business in that they have no obvious vested institutional interest to serve. What journalists frequently do not realize is that they have personally vested interest in the form of distinct political and economic views—views that place them not only to the left of business executives but of the general public as well.

Journalists live a rather sheltered life. They associate mostly with other journalists, they read mostly what other journalists write, and they have very little contact with the news-consuming public.[7] Business executives may lead an equally sheltered existence, with one difference—their daily confrontation with the news—and because their political and economic views differ so greatly from journalists, they are much more likely to be aware of media bias. This is not to deny that the ideal story for many, if not most, business executives would be a reprint of their latest press release; and while making CEOs happy and curing many headaches for PAEs, such "reporting" should not be seriously contemplated.

Still, journalists should recognize what business executives intuit, however vaguely. The public image of business is shaped to a significant extent by the news media. Journalists are not entirely neutral arbiters of reality since they must, of necessity, select and interpret reality and present it in a way that will be interesting and intelligible to the news-consuming public. It is in this process of selection, interpretation, and presentation that news distortion occurs. The news media is too important in a democracy for journalists to be complacent about their work or self-righteous when challenged. Entertainment can distort news content and give the public a false impression of reality. The personal political and economic views of reporters can influence the content of their stories. Only with a degree of self-consciousness and introspection uncommon among reporters can journalism be improved and the public better served.

NOTES

1. The literature is too extensive to list here, but see, for example, Craig E. Aronoff, ed., *Business and the Media* (Santa Monica, Cal.: Goodyear Publishing Company, 1979); Howard Simmons and Joseph A. Califano, Jr., eds., *The Media and Business* (New York: Random House, 1979); "Media vs. Business: A Symposium of Views," *Los Angeles Business and Economics*, Special Issue, Vol. 5, No. 2 (Spring, 1980); and A. Kent MacDougall, *Ninety Seconds to Tell It All* (Homewood, Ill.: Dow Jones-Irwin, 1981).

2. An important recent exception to this are the following works by Stanley Rothman and S. Robert Lichter: "Media and Business Elites," *Public Opinion*, Col. 4, No. 5 (October–November, 1981), pp. 42ff; "Media and Business Elites: Two Classes in Conflict?" *The Public Interest*, No. 69 (Fall, 1982), pp. 117-25; and "Are Journalists a New Class?" *Business Forum*, Vol. 8, No. 3 (Spring, 1983), pp. 12-17.

3. "Business Thinks TV Distorts Its Image," *Business Week* (October 18, 1982), p. 26.

4. In what follows, contingency tables and correlations are significant at the .05 level of confidence or better unless otherwise stated.

5. Stanley Rothman provides a useful summary and bibliography in "The Mass Media in Post-Industrial Society," in *The Third Century: America as a Post-Industrial Society*, ed. Seymour Martin Lipset (Stanford, Cal.: Hoover Institution Press, 1979), pp. 346-88.

6. Ibid., p. 352.

7. Stephen Hess, *The Washington Reporters* (Washington, D.C.: The Brookings Institution, 1981), pp. 1-23.

5

Business: Attacked from Without and Undermined from Within? The Role of Public Affairs

THE IMPORTANCE OF PUBLIC AFFAIRS

Many companies have responded to what is perceived as adverse coverage of business in the media by increasing the size and importance of their public affairs departments, in order to more effectively "market" the firm to the public.[1] This is accomplished in a variety of ways, from internally produced communcations to employees and shareholders to speeches to public groups; from news releases to op-ed pieces; and from testifying before the local planning commission to hiring full-time lobbyists in Washington, D.C. In all of this public affairs personnel are key because they are the ones who develop, implement, and advise senior management on proper corporate strategy.

Several analysts recently have questioned the performance of these PAEs, asserting that they tend to share the liberal, anti-business ideology of the press and tend to misrepresent and subvert business interests. For example, Robert L. Bartley, editor of the *Wall Street Journal*, has argued that the expansion of the public affairs function has resulted in business being infiltrated by its critics. The result, says Bartley, is that not only are business interests being attacked from without they are being undermined from within.[2] B. Bruce-Briggs, another advocate of this view, summarizes the argument:

Within the corporations are the line managers who direct production and distribution, but also the growing staffs in public affairs, government relations, internal education, and long-range planning, and in trade associations or research organizations who deal in ideas/words. These staffs look to the university (and to the media) as a reference group. They are not (or not yet?) a dominant element in the corporation, but they are growing in numbers and perhaps in influence.[3]

Since symbol manipulation is a primary component of the public affairs function, argues Bruce-Briggs, PAEs often have educational backgrounds and ideological inclinations more in common with the press than with line executives in the firm. Even those who have educational backgrounds in business often end up in public affairs because their careers in the line organization were derailed. Once in the public affairs slot, according to Bruce-Briggs, these executives reeducate "themselves by imbibing deeply from the wells of contemporary wisdom," which wisdom has been shaped by the antibusiness ideology of the new class.[4]

Whatever the cause, a variety of studies have documented the relatively liberal, antibusiness ideology of the press.[5] New recruits to journalism, with educational backgrounds in the more liberal, antibusiness disciplines, enter an occupational environment that generally reinforces this ideology. Line executives in business and industry, although having educational backgrounds in the more conservative, probusiness disciplines, similarly enter an occupational milieu that reinforces their ideology. But what of PAEs? They come from liberal, antibusiness disciplines but enter a conservative, probusiness milieu. This chapter examines the attitudes of journalists, PAEs, and CEOs on a variety of issues relating to business and the media, keeping in mind the peculiar situation of the PAE.

ATTITUDES TOWARD BUSINESS AND THE MEDIA

As noted above, an important function of public affairs is symbol manipulation. Thus, it is not surprising that PAEs tend to have degrees in the social sciences, humanities, and journalism rather than in business and engineering, as is typical of the line executives. The educational background of the PAEs is more likely

Table 5.1
Undergraduate Majors (row percent)

	Journalism	SS/Hum	Econ	Sci	Bus/Eng	(N)
Journalists	53	38	4	1	4	157
PAEs	26	40	5	6	23	217
CEOs	1	14	12	6	67	190

TOTAL   566

to resemble the journalist he communicates with than the CEO to whom he reports. Table 5.1 summarizes the educational backgrounds of the journalists, PAEs, and CEOs.

The differences, although predictable, are striking. More than one-quarter of the public affairs respondents reported undergraduate degrees in journalism, and 40 percent reported degrees in the social sciences or humanities. Only 23 percent reported degrees in business or engineering. Of the CEOs in our sample, only two individuals reported undergraduate degrees in journalism (both were heads of major publishing companies), only 14 percent reported degrees in the social sciences or humanities, while more than two-thirds (67 percent) reported degrees in business and engineering. Of the journalists, 53 percent reported degrees in journalism and another 38 percent in the social sciences or humanities. Only 4 percent reported degrees in business (none in engineering) and another 4 percent in economics.

Insofar as formal education and knowledge are correlated, the results presented in Table 5.1 support the view of business—that reporters lack knowledge about business and economic affairs. Also interesting to note is that the business reporters were no more likely to have degrees in business or economics than the general assignment reporters. Thus, whatever additional knowledge business reporters may have about business and economic affairs, it appears to be acquired "on the job" rather than through formal education.

The educational background of the PAEs gives at least prima facie support to the views of Bartley and Bruce-Briggs. Studies have shown that there is a correlation between educational background or discipline and political ideology, including attitudes toward business. Not only are faculty in the social sciences and humanities (which includes journalism) more liberal and critical of business than those in business and engineering, but students majoring in the various disciplines tend to share the faculty view, and student views more closely approximate faculty views as the student approaches graduation.[6] Thus, it is well documented that graduates with majors in the social sciences and humanities start their careers more liberal and critical of business than business and engineering graduates. The question is how their occupation affects their views.

At least since former budget director David Stockman's *Atlantic* interview, where he termed Reaganomics as traditional Republican "trickle down" theory, the debate about who will be the prime beneficiaries of Reagan's economic policies has been intense. The stated emphasis of the Reagan Administration has been to reduce regulation and taxes in order to increase productivity and saving. The claim is that the resulting economic growth will benefit all. In President Kennedy's metaphor, a rising tide lifts all boats. From this perspective, except for the "truly needy," entitlement programs should yield to programs that will stimulate growth. In this view, the poor ultimately will benefit more from their share of a growing economy than a larger share of a stagnant economy. Critics of Reaganomics retort that deregulation will result in damage to consumers and the environment and that reduced taxes will do little to stimulate growth. Existing entitlement programs, they say, offer only minimal protection to the poor and certainly should not be reduced. Furthermore, they would add, since tax reductions disproportionately benefit the rich and do little to increase productivity, financing for entitlement programs should come from higher taxes.

If the above description fairly represents the conservative supply-side position of the Reagan Administration and the opposing liberal, Keynesian position, we would expect it also to divide business executives and journalists. The following statement, included in the questionnaire, allowed this hypothesis to be tested: "President Reagan's economic policies will disproportionately benefit wealthy individuals and large corporations and do little to help the poor." Table 5.2 summarizes the responses.

Table 5.2
Reagan's Policies Will Benefit Wealthy, Not Poor (row percent)

	Strongly Agree	Agree with Reservations	Disagree with Reservations	Strongly Disagree	(N)
Journalists	35	42	14	9	161
PAEs	6	15	30	49	235
CEOs	2	6	29	62	205

The results indicate that the typical journalist and business executives are in strong disagreement over the effects of Reagan's policies. More than 77 percent of the journalists agree that Reagan's policies will disproportionately benefit wealthy individuals and large corporations compared to more than 89 percent of the CEOs who disagree! Note that the PAEs more closely resemble the CEOs than the journalists. Only 21 percent of the PAEs agreed with the statement compared to 79 percent who disagreed. The PAEs, however, do occupy an intermediate position between the journalist and CEO.

The same pattern emerges on a variety of other issues relating to business and economic policy and business-media relations. It is worthwhile to review some examples.

A prominent textbook on public relations includes loyalty to the employing organization as essential for effective public relations.[7] Corporate loyalty would seem to depend, at least in part, on the degree to which the individual is in accord with the basic objectives of the firm. The less agreement, other things being equal, the more difficult loyalty becomes. In any business the overriding objective is profit, but society considers the pursuit of profit legitimate only if it is believed to have a beneficial effect. In premodern or traditional societies, the pursuit of profit was discouraged because it was believed that economic gain for one person meant loss for another. This "zero sum" conception of economic exchange made the pursuit of profit antisocial.

In modern democratic, capitalist societies the mutually beneficial or "positive sum" character of economic exchange is recognized, thus legitimizing the pursuit of profit.[8] Still, no one would argue that all profit-seeking is mutually beneficial or that profit is an infallible guide to the public interest. (Many voluntary exchanges are ruled illegal precisely because there is a consensus that they do not further the public interest. Drug trafficking is an example.) In addition, one measure of support for capitalism is the degree to which an individual believes profit equals the public interest. In the terminology of the public relations textbook, the more convinced the individual is that profit equals the public interest the more likely he is to be loyal to the firm.

An item included in the survey helps test this proposition. Table 5.3 summarizes the responses to the statement "Increasingly the real interests of society and the profit interests of business are divergent." Of the three groups in the sample, the journalists are by far the most likely to doubt the coincidence of profit and the public interest, with 35 percent agreeing with the statement. By contrast, only 7 percent of the CEOs agree with the statement compared to 93 percent who disagree. The responses of the PAEs resemble the CEOs more closely than the journalists, but again they fall between the two, with 14 percent agreeing with the statement and 87 percent disagreeing.

Table 5.3
Interests of Society and Profit Interests Divergent (row percent)

	Strongly Agree	Agree with Reservations	Disagree with Reservations	Strongly Disagree	(N)
Journalists	10	25	50	16	161
PAEs	2	12	35	52	236
CEOs	3	4	31	62	205
				TOTAL	602

Consider another, related policy issue. To the extent that the market is considered an inadequate guide to the public interest, some alternative mechanism will be demanded. When it is perceived that the profit interests of business contradict the public interest, the most common demand is for government regulation. Table 5.4 summarizes responses to the following item: "To avoid

Table 5.4

Industry Must Be Closely Regulated (row percent)

	Strongly Agree	Agree with Reservations	Disagree with Reservations	Strongly Disagree	(N)
Journalists	4	45	38	14	162
PAEs	1	10	42	48	236
CEOs	2	3	37	59	206
				TOTAL	604

harm to the public, business must be closely regulated by government."

Again, the responses of the journalists differ significantly from those of the business executives. Almost half of the journalists agree that industry must be closely regulated, compared to just 11 percent of the PAEs and only 5 percent of the CEOs. While a bare majority (52 percent) of the journalists disagree on the need for close regulation, 90 percent of the PAEs disagree, and a near unanimous 95 percent of the CEOs disagree. Clearly, there is a vast difference of opinion between journalists and business executives on the need for regulation. Again, however, the PAEs were less likely than the CEOs to oppose regulation. There is this tentative support for the concerns expressed by Bartley and Bruce-Briggs that public affairs staff does not fully share the views of the line officers.

HOW TO DEAL WITH THE PRESS

The educational background of the PAEs more closely resembles that of the journalists than the CEOs. Considering the function performed by public affairs, this educational background is, of course, perfectly logical. We have seen that PAEs and CEOs differ on issues relating to business and economic policy; the next question is whether they also differ on business-media relations.

The study included a number of items dealing specifically with the role of the press. In comparing the responses of the three groups in our survey, each item revealed significant differences between the journalists and business executives in our sample, and most—but not all—differentiated the PAE from the CEO. One of these was in response to the statement "In general, business news reporting is not critical enough of business." Table 5.5 summarizes the responses.

Table 5.5
Reporters Not Critical Enough of Business (row percent)

	Strongly Agree	Agree with Reservations	Disagree with Reservations	Strongly Disagree	(N)
Journalists	17	47	32	4	160
PAEs	3	9	52	35	235
CEOs	1	6	40	53	206
				TOTAL	601

The general attitudes on press coverage of business by journalists and business executives is highlighted in response to this statement. Sixty-four percent of the journalists agreed that the press is not critical enough of business compared to 93 percent of the CEOs who disagreed. Clearly, the journalists and CEOs do not see eye to eye in this issue. The PAEs, while more closely resembling the CEOs than the journalists, again fall between the two. Although only 11 percent agree that the press is not critical enough of business, compared to 7 percent of the CEOs, the PAEs are much more reserved about the matter. Fifty-two percent of the PAEs disagree with reservations compared to 40 percent of the CEOs, and only 35 percent strongly disagree compared to 53 percent of the CEOs.

The more critical one is of business the more likely one is to believe that press coverage of business is not critical enough. This is reflected in the responses in Table 5.5; journalists, being most critical of business, are most likely to believe press coverage is not critical enough, with PAEs next, followed by the CEOs. The results again fit with the theory that PAEs constitute a Fifth Column within the corporation.

Consider responses to a final issue relating to the media. One of business's most frequently voiced criticisms of the press is that their attempt to be entertaining distorts news content. The reporter's preference for dramatic and unusual stories, these critics assert, makes them seem like common occurrences. Coverage given to illegal payments by U.S. multinational corporations to foreign governments, they contend, gives the public the impression that bribery is a typical business modus operandi. These business executives believe that reporters do not cover the many honest and legal business operations because they aren't considered "newsworthy." Journalists have retorted that, almost by definition, "news" is the unusual rather than the commonplace event and that reporting the routine would not attract or hold the interest of readers. The fundamental disagreement between business and the press in all of this is that business believes that news content is distorted by what it considers press sensationalism, and journalists deny, first, that it is sensationalism and, second, that there is significant distortion.

The following items confirm the basic disagreement. Table 5.6 summarizes responses to the following statement: "There is an element of entertainment to news reporting, and most reporters will choose the dramatic and unusual story over the commonplace and mundane." There is substantial agreement among all three groups that news reporting involves an element of entertainment. Eighty-six percent of the journalists agreed with the statement, as did 95 percent of the PAEs and 98 percent of the CEOs. The important difference, however, is that the journalists are considerably more reserved in their agreement than the business executives, just as the PAEs are more reserved than the CEOs.

If reporters tend to choose the dramatic and unusual story over the commonplace and mundane, what is the effect on news content? The following item helps answer that question: "An attempt to make news entertaining seriously distorts its content."

Table 5.6
Element of Entertainment to News Reporting (row percent)

	Strongly Agree	Agree with Reservations	Disagree with Reservations	Strongly Disagree	(N)
Journalists	32	54	11	4	161
PAEs	70	25	5	–	235
CEOs	76	22	2	–	206

| | | | | | TOTAL | 601 |

Note the differences between the journalists and business executives (see Table 5.7). One-fourth of the journalists agree with the statement compared to three-fourths of the CEOs and PAEs. Thus, both the PAEs and CEOs agree in virtually identical proportions that news content is distorted by the attempt to make it entertaining. This compares to three-fourths of the journalists who disagree.

The deep division between business and the media on this issue may very well be a function of the fact that the roles and responsibilities of reporters and business executives are quite different. The journalist must report the news and do it in such a way that people will want to read it. That there is an element of entertainment to news reporting does not make reporters entertainers, and they are loath to admit that entertainment supersedes content. In addition, reporters are not obliged to live with the consequences of the stories they write. Business executives, on the other hand, are not concerned with selling newspapers or attracting readers and are very sensitive about how they are portrayed in the press. They wish to be presented in the best possible light and must live with the consequences of anything less favorable. These different roles and responsibilities, it seems likely, are the source of this difference of opinion between journalists and business.

Table 5.7
Attempt to Entertain Distorts News Content (row percent)

	Strongly Agree	Agree with Reservations	Disagree with Reservations	Strongly Disagree	(N)
Journalists	7	18	55	21	160
PAEs	25	51	22	2	233
CEOs	26	51	22	2	200
				TOTAL	593

THE CASE FOR CORPORATE "MOLES"

In comparing the responses of journalists, PAEs, and CEOs to the several items relating to business and economic policy and the role of the press, remarkable differences of opinion are found. In general, journalists are comparatively critical of business, are more likely to believe that profit is not a reliable guide to the public interest, and feel that additional business regulation is necessary. At the same time, the journalists are more likely than the business executives to defend press coverage of business. They do not think that the press is too critical of business—almost two-thirds believe that it is not critical enough—and they believe that press criticism and coverage of dramatic and unusual events does not distort news content.

On all of these issues business executives disagreed with the journalists—in most cases quite sharply—and in all of the cases except one, the opinion of the PAEs differed from the CEOs in the direction of the journalists. The results, in other words, offer some support for the views of Bartley and Bruce-Briggs that PAEs may be (in spy talk) "corporate moles."

However, the reasons ordinarily given to explain this phenomenon do not bear scrutiny. Everett Carll Ladd, Jr., among others, has argued that education—almost without regard to discipline—is responsible for the increasingly liberal, antibusiness attitudes among the formerly more conservative, probusiness middle class. Education, he says, which produces this "new liberalism," overwhelms occupational categories, and "when education is held constant, the occupation-related differences disappear completely."[9]

Comparing attitudes of business and journalism students at two major universities, Rothman and Lichter found that the journalism students are considerably more liberal and critical of business than business executives.[10] The conclusion drawn from these and similar observations is that education is undermining the business system, first, by producing nonbusiness professionals and managers—such as journalists—who are very critical of business, and, second, by producing business executives who are not committed to the values of the institutions that employ them. The PAEs are but one, albeit very conspicuous, example.

If Bartley and Bruce-Briggs are correct, the PAEs in many U.S. corporations may be marketing the wrong product, unwittingly supported by senior management. Instead of representing, explaining, and advocating business interests as perceived and defined by management, PAEs may be misrepresenting and undermining those interests. This survey cannot determine how adequately PAEs actually represent the interests of their employers, but it does assess their attitudes on some important issues relating to business and economic policy and business-media relations and compare them with the attitudes of journalists and CEOs. These comparisons allow a more considered evaluation of allegations of Bartley and Bruce-Briggs.

I would be more sanguine about the future of the business system. Although the PAEs do differ marginally from the CEOs in the direction of the journalists, the difference, though in most cases statistically significant, is quite small. Surprisingly, academic discipline has little effect on attitudes. That is, PAEs who reported degrees in typically liberal, antibusiness disciplines were not significantly more likely to be critical of business than those who reported degrees in business. This may be explained partly by self-selection. Attitude toward business is likely to influence career choice, with those more favorably disposed toward business most likely to choose careers in corporate public affairs.

However, if discipline does not account for the differences between PAEs and CEOs, what does? The answer, quite simply, is age. The PAEs have a median age of 47.7 years compared to 55.8 years for the CEOs. When age is held constant, virtually all the differences between the two groups disappeared.

Age is important for two reasons. First, people tend to become more conservative with age. (This was also true for the journalists. Controlling for age, however, did not reduce the attitudinal differences between journalists and business executives.)

Second, and potentially more important, the longer an individual is with a corporation or in the private sector, the more likely he will be to identify with the interests of business. Although a question was not included that enabled a direct test of this hypothesis, it is likely that there is a strong correlation between age and tenure. The older the respondent, the longer he is likely to have been in corporate public affairs and the more likely he is to identify with the interests of business. When the PAEs and CEOs forty-five years and older were compared (there were not enough CEOs under forty-five for a statistically valid comparison), the responses were indistinguishable.

The implications for management are twofold. First, the huge difference of opinion between business executives and journalists on issues relating to business and the media helps explain the business executive's perennial complaint about bad press. Business executives traditionally have been quite naive about press relations. When they haven't treated press inquiry as a form of snooping into private business affairs, they have felt that unfavorable press coverage was essentially a communications problem; if journalists only understood business and economic affairs better, press coverage would surely improve. No doubt better understanding would result in more informed press coverage, but it is unlikely that it would do much to reduce the fundamental differences of opinion documented in our study. Business executives should recognize that journalists do not share their view on many important issues relating to business and economic policy, and they should plan accordingly rather than to operate under the (perhaps more comforting) illusion that it is all a problem of misunderstanding.

Second, the attitudes of journalists toward business highlight the necessity for effective public affairs. Although the younger PAEs may not fully share management's views on issues relating to business and economic policy and business media relations, the difference is relatively small and tends to disappear with age. The difference exists, nevertheless, and management should recognize the potential for conflict between the personal beliefs of PAEs and corporate interests. If such a conflict occurs, it is unlikely that corporate interests will be represented optimally. When staffing the public affairs department, therefore, it is prudent, particularly when considering younger applicants or applicants who have not been employed previously in corporate public affairs, to be sure that the individual is clear on what issues are involved and what is expected. It is prudent, also, that management not abdicate its responsibility for overseeing the development and execution of public affairs policy. This policy is too important to be left entirely in the hands of the public affairs staff.

NOTES

1. I use the term "public affairs" synonymously with public relations, external affairs, and like terms. The function includes relations with external groups, such as the press, politicians, citizen groups, and so on, as well as some internal relations, such as employee and shareholder communications.

2. Robert L. Bartley, "Business and the New Class," in *The New*

Class?, ed. B. Bruce-Briggs (New Brunswick, N.J.: Transaction Books, 1979), pp. 64-65.

3. B. Bruce-Briggs, "Conclusion: Notes Toward a Delineation of the New Class" in Ibid., p. 207.

4. Ibid.

5. S. Robert Lichter and Stanley Rothman, "The Media and Business Elites," *Public Opinion*, Vol. 4, No. 5 (October–November, 1981), pp. 42-46, 59-60; John W. C. Johnstone, Edward J. Slawski, and William W. Bowman, *The New People* (Chicago: University of Chicago Press, 1976), pp. 92-93.

6. For academic attitudes see Fred J. Evans, "Toward a Theory of Academic Liberalism," *Journal of Politics*, Vol. 42, No. 4 (November, 1980), pp. 993-1030; for values associated with recruitment to academic discipline see Morris Rosenberg, *Occupations and Values* (Glencoe, Ill.: The Free Press, 1957).

7. Scott M. Cutlip and Allen H. Center, *Effective Public Relations* (Englewood Cliffs, N.J.: Prentice-Hall, Inc., 1982), pp. 44-45.

8. Michael Novak makes this point brilliantly in *The Spirit of Democratic Capitalism* (New York: American Enterprise Institute/Simon & Schuster, 1982).

9. Everett Carll Ladd, Jr., "Pursuing the New Class: Social Theory and Survey Data," in *The New Class?*, ed. B. Bruce-Briggs (New Brunswick, N.J.: Transaction Books, 1979), p. 118.

10. Stanley Rothman and S. Robert Lichter, "Are Journalists a New Class?," *Business Forum*, Vol. 8, No. 2 (Spring, 1983), pp. 12-17.

6

Understanding Differences
and Using Them to Advantage

FIVE POINTS IN REVIEW

The discussion of business and the media thus far has focused on five major points: (1) the different worldviews of business executives and journalists; including (2) their divergent political orientations; (3) their different positions on business and economic issues; and (4) their different views on the roles and responsibilities of the press; and (5) the extent of press bias in reporting business and economic news.

This chapter will review each of these points before drawing some conclusions on how business can best deal with the media.

1. *Divergent worldviews*. Business executives and journalists are far apart in how they view the world. Both groups are highly educated; most have bachelor's degrees and many have advanced degrees. However, the educational experiences of the two groups are quite different. Journalists typically have undergraduate degrees in the social sciences or humanities, most often English, history, political science, or journalism. The values associated with these disciplines include the desire to help people, to be intellectually creative, and to be politically liberal. Many of the students who enter these disciplines share the values associated with them, and many more come to share them by the time they graduate. Upon graduation, they enter an occupational environment that reinforces these values.

Business executives, by contrast, typically have undergraduate degrees in business or engineering and advanced degrees in business or law. The values associated with these disciplines include a strong achievement orientation, the desire to make money, and conservatism. Like the journalists, many of these future business executives begin college sharing these values, and many more come to share them by graduation. Once they enter the world of business the values are reinforced.

Thus, business executives and journalists begin with different orientations and pursue educational and career paths that reinforce them. The exceptions to this are the public affairs/public relations executives who often begin their studies and sometimes their careers as journalists and who later enter the business world. As seen in Chapter 4, the attitudes of PAEs differ from those of other business executives in the direction of the journalists. Occupational environment is a powerful force for socialization, however, and the longer these executives work in business the more closely their views match that of other executives.

2. *Political differences.* The politics of the press and business are quite different. Journalists are considerably to the left of the general public and business executives to the right. Journalists usually think of themselves as Democrats and typically vote Democratic. Business executives are staunchly Republican in their party identification and vote thus.

These political differences stem, in part, from the divergent interests that the two groups represent. Business represents the traditional establishment and traditional values. Journalists represent the new class or intelligentsia and the emerging power and influence of the "knowledge industry." The Republican Party—long identified as the party of business, the middle class, and traditional values—is the natural vehicle for the political interests of business. The Democratic Party, since the New Deal, has been identified as the party of labor and minorities in opposition to the more privileged establishment, including business. As such, it is the natural vehicle for the political interests of the new class in general and journalists in particular. The different political affiliations of business and the media reflect a certain amount of competition and a degree of hostility between these two "establishments."

3. *Business and economic issues.* The concept of a self-regulating economic system is difficult to comprehend intellectually and to accept politically. The great contribution of economics has been to explain how the independent decisions of millions of producers and consumers can be coordinated through the market in such a way that the goods and services desired by consumers will be provided by producers at a price that approximates the actual cost of production. No central individual, agency, party, or government is needed to tell people what to consume or what to produce. What is more, over the long run the free exchange of goods and services makes everybody better off. This is one of the most profound insights in modern social thought, and it provides the justification for capitalism as an economic system.

Yet, once said this statement must be qualified immediately. The market is an accurate signal only when there is competition. Restraints of trade, whatever the source, distort the market. The role of government should be to prevent these restraints. In addition, the market does not take into account externalities, or costs, imposed on third parties. Probably the most notorious of these externalities is pollution. Preventing or minimizing such externalities provides another justification for government intervention.

Finally, the market is amoral but society is moral. Every society has rules governing what transactions are appropriate or legitimate. There is, for example, a market for murder, and some people do hire others to kill, but society considers such transactions illegitimate and hence criminal. On a more mundane level, most cities have parklands that are intentionally excluded from commercial development. In these and similar cases government intervention is needed to restrict the scope of the market.

Within contemporary society there exists simultaneously the belief that individuals ought to be allowed to pursue their economic interests without interference from government and the belief that government ought to intervene to regulate or to prohibit particular transactions. Nonintervention presupposes that the interests of the individual and society are harmoniously coordinated by the market. Intervention recognizes that the market is an imperfect coordinator and that some things should be excluded from it.

Many studies have demonstrated that there is a strong relationship between general political orientation—liberal or conservative, Democrat or Republican—and belief in the necessity of government intervention in the economy. The more liberal the individual, the more likely he will be to believe that the market is an imperfect coordinator of individual economic activity and that there is a greater need for active government intervention in the economy. The more conservative the individual the more likely he is to believe that government intervention is not needed and may even be harmful.

Journalists are in general quite skeptical of the view that the market adequately disciplines business so that its interests and those of the public are consistent. Thus, journalists tend to favor increased regulation and control of business. Business executives naturally feel that their interests and the interests of their firm in particular and business in general are consistent with the public interest. Rather than more regulation, most business executives feel that less regulation is needed. The views of both groups are more extreme than that of the general public. Journalists characteristically favor more regulation than the public and business executives less; journalists are more critical of business than the public, business executives less critical.

4. *Role of the press.* That business executives are conservative and have great confidence in the idea that the interests of business and the larger society are consistent is not surprising. As journalists often point out, business executives are merely expressing a view consistent with their own interests—but what of journalists and journalism? Journalists typically think of themselves as public servants not influenced, as are others, by vested interests.

When the views of journalists on the adequacy of news coverage are examined, however, they tend to be quite defensive—almost as if they were defending a special interest. Journalists do not believe that competition between news sources adversely affects news quality or that the need to be entertaining has any distorting effect on news content. In addition, most reporters remain convinced that, whatever their personal views, their reporting remains unbiased and objective. Whether in fact true or not, their views are consistent with the vested interests of the media just as the views of business executives are consistent with the interests of business.

5. *Media bias.* That journalists hold views consistent with their interests raises the question of media bias. In a technical sense, no

one is totally unbiased. Psychologists remind us that people must learn to perceive reality, and how they learn affects what they see. In a practical sense, however, we can all agree that there is such a thing as objective reality and can agree on what it is. The disagreement comes when facts are ambiguous or must be interpreted and when deciding what is newsworthy and what is not.

Although studies of the media, including those reported in this book, provide circumstantial evidence supporting the case for media bias, none has systematically established that case. Chapters 2 and 3 showed that the attitudes of journalists can lead to biased reporting; and various other studies, such as those sponsored by the Media Institute, have shown that the media do not present a balanced view on particular issues. However, there has been very little direct evidence linking the attitudes of journalists with the imperatives of the medium to systematically explain media bias. Without this information, all that is possible is informed speculation.

Given the political and economic views of journalists, it would be extraordinary if news coverage were not exceptionally critical of business. Now this does not mean that journalists are consciously more critical of business or business executives than other institutions or individuals. It is more that there is an underlying presumption against business. Business executives have an extra burden of proof to establish the purity of their motives and the consistency of their interests with that of the public's. The following illustrates this point.

Several years ago I invited the then-editor of the business section of one of the nation's largest newspapers to speak on business and the media to a class I was teaching. During the course of his presentation, he made two telling comments reflecting his attitude toward business. The first was that when Ralph Nader came on the scene, he said, "we [journalists] thought of him as one of our own." The second comment was that when he thought of the Soviet state bureaucracy he thought of it as crushing individuality with ruthless abandon. In this respect, he said, the large corporation reminded him of the Soviet bureaucracy. Given such attitudes, the presumption is on the side of the critics of business, and unless they are proven wrong beyond doubt, their views will be given prominence in the news.

In addition to what may be called the ideological bias in news reporting, there is a bias associated with the medium in which the news is presented.

All news presented in the mass media of communication—newspapers, television, radio—must be presented in such a way as to attract an audience. Network news, in part because of the intense competition between networks for viewers, has become as much entertainment as news; but in all the media there is an effort to entertain by pointing out the unusual, the unexpected, and the shocking. News must be presented in such a way that it will attract the attention of the average person who is uninformed and has no prior interest in the topic. Thus, the medium focuses news reporting not just on the most important events but frequently on the most dramatic events, regardless of their importance. This explains why bad news is so often featured over good news and why the less interesting or more complex stories are avoided.

TOWARD A MORE EFFECTIVE MEDIA STRATEGY

From what has been said thus far, the outline of an effective media strategy can be developed.

1. *Emphasize the consistency of business and the public interest.* The interests of business and the public in general are quite consistent, but beware of the zero sum argument. In the zero sum argument, profits reflect the exploitation of workers or consumers. In any case, profits are gained at the expense of society. In the positive sum argument, profits reflect the efficient offering of a product or service that people desire. Instead of society being worse off it is better off. Thus, in referring to business achievements be careful to emphasize how society also benefits.

When Mobil Oil Company acquired Reliance Electric, such an argument was made. When the merger was announced, oil companies were in disfavor because of high prices and profits resulting from the Iranian Revolution. Mobil anticipated adverse press and public reaction and emphasized in its press conference how the merger would allow research and development of a new, more energy efficient electric motor. The clear implication was that society as a whole would benefit from the transaction.

2. *Remember your audience.* Ultimately, the audience of business is the public, not the press. The views of the public are quite

different from that of the media, but they are also different from that of business. The message communicated should be formulated so that it will appeal to its ultimate audience.

In the case of Mobil Oil, the press was likely to be more critical than the public about the merger, and it was important that management be able to present its case clearly to the public. If the press conference had not been held, and had the press learned about the merger from independent sources, the press and not Mobil Oil would have set the agenda for the story. Mobil would have been contacted about the story but with such likely questions as "Why isn't Mobil using its profits to find more oil?" or "Why were you trying to hide the proposed merger?" By holding the press conference before the news reached the press, Mobil was able to set the agenda by determining the content of the conference. This press strategy allowed Mobil to communicate its message that the merger was good because it would benefit the public.

3. *Communicate through the press.* The objective of press communications is not to influence press opinion but public opinion. To do this, however, business executives must understand how journalists think. Journalists think of themselves as public interest advocates, and they view business as a special interest oftentimes at odds with the public interest. Thus, it is important that business couch its message in terms of the public interest. In doing so, however, it should not be implied that business's interests are indistinguishable from the public's, because they are not and no journalist will believe they are. The points to emphasize are the basic integrity of the firm and how in each particular case the interests of the firm and the public are compatible.

To do more than demonstrate the consistency of interests in a particular instance, that is, to attempt to educate the press so that it will come to view business as business executives do, is ultimately futile. Mobil Oil was able to minimize negative comments on the merger by emphasizing the public benefits of that particular transaction, not by convincing the press that it had a right to do what it did.

4. *Establish credibility—not friendship.* Again, the idea is not to convert journalists to the business point of view but to convince them that you are a reliable and credible source of information. The possibility of changing a journalist's basic attitudes toward business is remote at best. Fortunately, journalists do not have to

be converted, only informed. If journalists feel that you are a good and reliable source of information, the message you present to them will be relayed by them to the public with a minimal amount of distortion. When they have a question or need a quote, they will call. This does not require a policy of total openness, but it does require access and honesty.

5. *The medium is the message.* Both journalists and business executives recognize that there is an element of entertainment to news reporting. However, business executives tend to eschew it in their communications because they think it distorts and distracts. The result is less media interest. Business should recognize that oftentimes how something is said is as important as what is said. Indirect and vague responses are not as newsworthy as clear and concise responses. Quotes and interviews from senior officers are more newsworthy than from junior officers. For television especially, the more articulate the individual the more newsworthy he is. Finding the most newsworthy individual to quote or be interviewed is frequently the best way to communicate the firm's message.

6. *The unusual is usual.* For the press, almost by definition, news is the unusual event. That is why business news is considered undesirable by most reporters. Most business news is relatively straightforward and predictable. Stock tables appear in the newspapers every day, and the best business news is good news. "Unemployment is down, profits are up" is good news but not as newsworthy as "Pockets of unemployment remain despite recovery."

Thus, in communicating with the press it is best to attempt to find an unusual angle to a story. Instead of reporting that profits are up in the second quarter, followed by an array of numbers, try a human interest approach. "Dr. West developed a new welding technique that contributed to second-quarter profits."

CONCLUDING COMMENTS

The intent of this chapter has been to summarize the findings presented in the first section of the book. The above comments on how to deal with the press are intended to be suggestive rather than conclusive. Certainly, they are not intended to provide a guide for a comprehensive media relations policy. Rather, they are intended to get the reader to comprehend the differences that exist between business and the media and the public, and to deal with them realistically rather than to assume these differences away or try to change them.

The remainder of the book will focus on case studies of business-media relations. Some of these cases involve crisis communications, others how business can use the media to its advantage. These cases allow some more practical lessons to be drawn. The survey and cases together are intended to provide a basis for a comprehensive understanding of business-media relations.

II
Case Studies and Conclusions

7

Crisis Communications at Seafirst: An Open-Door Policy

THE CRISIS

On Thursday, July 1, 1982, the *American Banker* carried a story stating that Bill G. Patterson, vice-president and chief energy lending officer at Penn Square, a small "shopping center" bank in Oklahoma, had been stripped of his lending authority. The story also reported that Penn Square executives were frantically seeking a $30 million capital infusion. In addition, legal action was being initiated seeking a temporary injunction to prevent Penn Square from terminating letters of credit on several gas and oil drilling operations. The Federal Reserve, the Comptroller of the Currency, and the FDIC received copies of the *American Banker* story. So did Seattle First-National Bank. The news was of special concern to Seafirst executives because the bank had participated in many of the loans originated by Penn Square.

At 2:30 P.M. that same day Penn Square officials publicly confirmed that some of their energy loans had become problems, thus confirming the *American Banker* story. Shortly thereafter, Seafirst issued a press release (see Exhibit 7.1) containing the following:

Seafirst Corporation acknowledged today that it has participated in loans with Penn Square Bank of Oklahoma. The Comptroller of the Currency recently identified certain Penn Square loans as problems. Penn Square's lending is under review, including all participant loans. The extent of the impact on Seafirst is not yet known.

Exhibit 7.1
Seafirst Press Releases

Partial text of press releases dated July 1, July 6, and July 13 indicate Seafirst's deteriorating financial situation. No one at Seafirst knew at the beginning how serious its financial situation would become. Note in the July 13 release the statement of financial condition with the attempt to reassure depositors and borrowers.

July 1, 1982
Seafirst Corporation acknowledged today that it has participated in loans with Penn Square Bank of Oklahoma. The Comptroller of the Currency recently identified certain Penn Square loans as problems. Penn Square's lending is under review, including all participant loans. The extent of the impact on Seafirst is not yet known.

July 6, 1982
Following the announcement by the Comptroller of the Currency that it was closing Penn Square Bank of Oklahoma City, Seafirst Corporation today made the following statement:

Seafirst Corporation is analyzing its participation in problem loans with Penn Square Bank. The analysis completed thus far indicates a large increase in loan losses, requiring an addition to the provision expense for loan losses.

The impact of any loan losses on second-quarter earnings has not yet been fully determined, but it appears that the quarter will show a loss. The first half of 1982 will still be profitable.

July 13, 1982
Seafirst Corporation is continuing to analyze the effects of its participation in problem loans originated by Penn Square Bank of Oklahoma.

Further review of participation loans from Penn Square and other energy credits has resulted in a decision to increase Seafirst's provision for loan losses in second quarter 1982 by an additional $125 million, $68 million after taxes. This decision is based on a review which is not fully complete. Completion of the analysis may indicate the need for further additions to the loan loss provision in the second half. It is management's current estimate that any further additions will not exceed approximately $40 million, $22 million after taxes. Management believes these estimates should be sufficient to cover all potential losses from the Penn Square situation and they have not been reduced to include potential recoveries.

> The increase in the provision for loan losses will result in a net operating loss for the second quarter and first half of 1982. Earlier, Seafirst had reported that it had anticipated a profitable first half of 1982.

This first press release foretold Seafirst's determination to be open with the press. The press release was criticized by the federal regulators and other banks that had participated in Penn Square loans for revealing too much too soon. The next day, investors reacted to the news by selling stock in banks that had participated in Penn Square loans. On July 5, 1982, Penn Square bank was declared insolvent and placed in receivership with the FDIC.

The decision to liquidate Penn Square and not to rescue its uninsured depositors was to have a devastating effect on Seafirst. It was a sign that bank examiners had tightened up on energy loans and loan portfolios. Without federal protection, Seafirst found itself locked out of the uninsured CD market.

On July 15, 1982, John R. Boyd, head of Seafirst's energy department, and his boss, John W. Nelson, executive vice-president in charge of Seafirst's World Banking Group, were fired. Under Nelson and Boyd, the energy department had participated in some $400 million worth of energy loans with Penn Square. Although Nelson ultimately was in charge, it was Boyd who was most often credited with responsibility for negotiating Seafirst's participation in the loans. Shortly thereafter, a federal grand jury assembled in Seattle and placed Boyd under investigation.

On August 19, 1982, William M. Jenkins announced his retirement as chairman of Seafirst, a post he had held since 1962. Jenkins is said to have created the climate, by promoting growth above all, in which his subordinates would pursue the questionable loans. After the initial disclosure of Seafirst's participation in Penn Square loans and the firing and resignation of important Seafirst executives, the crisis continued to deepen as awareness of the extent of the losses grew. On December 22, 1982, Joseph R. Curtis, a Seafirst vice-chairman, resigned, and Richard Jaehning, president, took early retirement.

Later that same month the Seafirst board of directors hired

Richard Cooley, the respected head of San Francisco-based Wells Fargo Bank, to head up the beleaguered institution. By Cooley's own account, he had no idea of the extent of the company's financial troubles when he accepted the position.

In late January, 1983, Seafirst announced a 1982 operating loss of $90.2 million, mostly the result of bad energy loans associated with Penn Square. The bank also announced that it had arranged a $1.5 billion "safety net" of commitments from the nation's thirteen largest banks. Simultaneously, Seafirst executives indicated that they would be willing to sell anything of value to help make up the bank's losses, from its downtown Seattle headquarters office building to its subsidiaries.

Saturday afternoon, April 23, Seafirst chairman Richard Cooley told the board of directors that the bank had sustained yet another loss of $133 million in the first quarter. This was much more than almost anyone would have imagined just a few months earlier (see Exhibit 7.2). The silver lining on this black cloud was that an agreement had been reached with Bank of America to purchase Seafirst for $200 million and to provide an immediate $200 million capital infusion. Soon after, the Washington State Legislature passed a bill allowing the merger, and what could have become the biggest bank failure to date instead became the biggest bank takeover (see Exhibit 7.3).

Exhibit 7.2
More Bad News

May 19, 1983
   Seafirst Corporation today suspended its dividend to shareholders for Second Quarter 1983. The dividend has been set at 12 cents per share for the previous quarter.

During the negotiations with Bank of America to purchase Seafirst, one of the most difficult public relations problems of the entire crisis arose. To complete the merger, legislation had to be enacted by the state allowing a state-chartered bank to be purchased by an out-of-state bank. This legislation was opposed by Rainier Bank, the state's second largest bank, among others. Sea-

Exhibit 7.3
Some Good News: The Merger with BankAmerica

June 10, 1983

The proposed merger of Seafirst Corp. with BankAmerica Corporation presents many great opportunities for the economic and community needs of the Pacific Northwest. To discuss the importance of the merger to the local area, Richard P. Cooley, Seafirst chairman, and Samuel Armacost, president and CEO of BankAmerica, have invited several hundred community and business leaders to lunch on Thursday, June 16. The event will start at 11:45A.M. at the Westin Hotel, Grand Ballroom III.

first's chief lobbyist, Joe Brennan, was sent to Olympia, Washington, to tell legislators how the bank's survival depended on passage of the legislation. Meanwhile, in Seattle, Cooley attempted to assuage the fears of investors, depositors, and the public by telling them that everything was in control.

Finally, on July 1, 1983, the Bank of America merger was approved by the shareholders. The crisis finally ended.

AN OPEN PRESS STRATEGY

As will be seen in Chapter 8, the press strategy employed by Beckman Instruments fell toward the closed end of a closed-to-open spectrum. The Seafirst strategy fell toward the open end. The reasons for this include the nature of the banking industry, the philosophy of the public relations staff, and the character of the issue.

Banks have long been regarded as conservative institutions with an organizational culture to match. Protected and controlled by federal and state regulations, competition between institutions was highly circumscribed. Banks were mildly profitable, low-risk operations, and since the banking regulations enacted in the wake of the Great Depression, bank failures were almost unknown. The recent deregulation of financial institutions changed all of this. Now there was competition not only between banks but between banks and savings and loans and banks and other nonbanking financial institutions. Rather abruptly, the real world of competition thrust itself into the genteel world of banking.

Deregulation forced banks to develop more aggressive marketing strategies and to pay more attention to public opinion. The increased emphasis on marketing and a concern for public opinion led to a greater willingness to be responsive to the press, particularly among institutions with a broad base of depositors.

Seafirst was affected by these industrywide trends. As the state's largest bank, it had high public visibility even before deregulation. In addition, Seafirst always seemed particularly sensitive to its rivalry with Rainier Bank, the state's second largest institution. In addition, C. M. "Mike" Berry, who was president from 1975 until his retirement in December, 1981, was very concerned about the public image of the bank and relied heavily on the corporate communications and community relations departments to help create and preserve that image. By the time his successor, Richard Jaehning—who was more of a traditional, internally oriented banker—became president, the organizational culture had become more explicitly concerned with public image, and the public relations department had establshed the philosophy of being open with the press.

Although in the long run the press philosophy of the public relations department must conform to the culture of the organization, in the short run that philosophy can be very important in shaping press strategy. In a crisis, the judgment of the public relations staff is relied upon heavily by management.

Art Merrick, vice-president and manager of corporate communications at Seafirst, epitomized the commitment to open press relations. As he put it, by being open with the press, even when the news is unfavorable, "We can position the story. And taking the initiative helps develop credibility with the press." Merrick's attitude was not so much that a company should bare its soul to the press as that by being open the company's message can be more effectively communicated. Katie Weiss, assistant vice-president for corporate communications, had just received her bachelor's degree in communications from the University of Washington when she accepted the position at Seafirst. Her view was that it was best to be totally open with the press, and by and large the reporters I talked with had a great deal of confidence in her. (She told reporters that her position with management was that if the right questions were asked, she would answer with the truth—even if it was something they did not want to see printed. Therefore, if there was something management did not want the press to know, they shouldn't tell her!) Randy James was a senior vice-president in charge of corporate affairs, of which corporate communications was one department. James came from personnel and had little formal training or experience in public relations prior to assuming his new position. He was considered part of senior management and reported directly to the president and was part of the management committee. Still, James adhered to what he called an "open door" policy on press relations.

Thus, the philosophy of the public relations staff was to be open, and throughout the crisis openness was encouraged. As Merrick put it, "We were engaged in a continual process of management education." By and large the philosophy of openness carried the day.

The nature of the issues made an open press strategy the best alternative. Seafirst was not the only source of information. The press knew of the bad loans that Seafirst had participated in with Penn Square almost as soon as Seafirst did. It would have been impossible for Seafirst to have kept its involvement hidden from the press. Seafirst also needed to be concerned that investors and depositors did not get exaggerated or misleading reports on the bank's condition.

It was feared that without comment by Seafirst the press would speculate and make the situation appear worse than it actually was. In addition, there was a real danger that the bank could lose deposits, not just the uninsured CDs, but the smaller insured deposits as well. There was a definite possibility that inaccurate or misleading press coverage could cause an old-fashioned run on the bank. Thus, Seafirst acutely felt the need to assure depositors that their funds were safe. The best way to do this was to maintain a relatively open relationship with the press.

In addition, the way the story unfolded, with each announcement and press release revealing ever more serious problems, was beguiling to both the press and Seafirst management. Although one reporter who covered the case disagrees, I am convinced that Seafirst management—much less the public relations staff—never imagined the extent of financial exposure the bank was to face. Originally, loan losses are estimated to be 40 million, then $125 million, and finally $483 million; much of Seafirst senior management is fired or forced into early retirement; a new CEO arrives and conducts an audit that reveals the bank is insolvent; a purchase by an out-of-state bank is arranged, but state banking laws must be changed; the laws are changed and the purchase is concluded. Each event seemed conclusive. Yet each event foreshadowed another, often more serious, event. Thus, each time the press was contacted with a major new development, the feeling was that—as bad as the news might be—this will be the last of it, and there was little to be gained by trying to hide information from the press.

In sum, the organizational culture of the bank and the philosophy of the public relations department was consistent with the kind of press relations the situation demanded, and the overall strategy and implementation was considered a success by the Seafirst staff involved.

PRESS RESPONSE

Seafirst's involvement with Penn Square was treated as big news by the press from the very outset. A small shopping center bank had gotten in over its head in questionable energy loans. Many of the loans made by Penn Square were sold to other banks, with Seafirst being a major purchaser. Heady times in the energy industry prevailed when the loans were made. Oil prices had skyrocketed in 1979 and were thought to be headed inexorably upward for the foreseeable future. However, the artificially high prices created by the OPEC cartel and the elimination of price controls on oil in the United States combined to produce new supplies. As the new supplies came on stream, and as price-induced conservation began to reduce demand, the price of crude oil began to soften. The collateral used to secure many of the loans—the undiscovered oil in the ground—lost value. As a consequence, a large number of the energy loans in Seafirst's portfolio had to be written off. Each price decline resulted in more bad loans for Seafirst.

Seafirst entered the energy lending business naively. John Boyd, who headed Seafirst's energy division, had no previous experience with energy loans. Boyd, however, was given support and encouragement by Bill Jenkins, chairman and CEO, who saw the loans as a means of achieving the growth he desired.

The first public notice of Seafirst's pending loan problems came in an *American Banker* article by Philip Zweig. Zweig was covering the Penn Square story but noted in passing that several other banks, among them Seafirst, had purchased many potentially bad loans from Penn Square. Greg Heberlein, a business reporter for the *Seattle Times*, picked up on the *American Banker* story and made a contact with an informant in the energy department at Seafirst. Although the informant's name was never revealed, Heberlein developed a list of nineteen points from the interview and confronted Seafirst with them. Heberlein's initial official contact was with Randy James. James, Heberlein said, did not or could not respond adequately to the points raised. Heberlein was then put in contact with Richard Jaehning, Seafirst president, who was able to respond to Heberlein's satisfaction. The resulting story marked the beginning of Heberlein's coverage for the *Seattle Times*. The day after the first story on Seafirst appeared in the *Seattle Times*, the *Seattle Post-Intelligencer* (*PI*) ran its first story. The article was written by Pam Leven, a *PI* business reporter. Throughout the affair, the most complete coverage was by Heberlein at the *Times* and Leven at the *PI*, although there also was coverage by the *American Banker*, the *Wall Street Journal*, and several television stations (see Exhibit 7.4).

In general, the reporters who covered the Seafirst story say they were satisfied with their access to people and information. Only one reporter with whom I spoke remained convinced after the fact that at least a few of the senior officers knew the extent of the financial damage from the beginning but refused to admit it publicly. Even this reporter, however, believed that the public relations staff was not privy to such information and held back relatively little.

Most of the reporters felt that Weiss and Merrick were most open and helpful, although they sometimes did not have enough information. A few commented that James was somewhat less helpful, that he seemed more concerned about protecting management. Interestingly, the reporters were unanimous in their feeling that when they did have an opportunity to talk to senior management these executives were quite open. This occurred in part because senior management was prepared to meet the press.

At least two "impromptu" interviews were arranged with top bank officers. Here is how one interview occurred. Pam Leven, the *PI* reporter, told how one day she was having lunch with Katie Weiss in the Seafirst cafeteria. Just after they sat down, Bill

Exhibit 7.4
Seafirst Headlines: Headlines Relating to the Crisis

Some of Penn Square's $2 Billion of Loans Sold to Bank Have
Become Problem Ones
Wall Street Journal, 7/2/82

Seafirst faces loss on problem loans
Seattle Times, 7/2/82

Small-bank failure gives Seafirst a jolt
Seattle PI, 7/7/82, page one

Seafirst to lay off up to 400 employees
Seattle Times, 7/15/82, page one

Two Seafirst aides resign in aftermath of Penn failure
Seattle Times, 7/16/82

Seafirst reports $56 million loss after bank failure
Seattle PI, 7/16/82

Seafirst summoned to Penn Square hearings
Seattle PI, 9/15/82

'Big red 1' paying a price for errors
Seattle Times, 5/8/83

Big cash depositors are leaving Seafirst
Seattle PI, 5/13/83

Jenkins, the chairman, walked in and sat down alone at another table. Weiss suggested that they ask to join him for lunch, which they did. Jenkins began talking about Seafirst's problems, and Leven began asking questions and taking notes. The result was an exclusive interview with Jenkins that appeared in the *PI*. When I asked Weiss about this incident, she indicated that it had all been arranged previously and that she later arranged a similar interview for Heberlein at the *Times* with Richard Jaehning. This proved an excellent way to give a reporter an exclusive interview, avoiding the necessity of holding a press conference and not appearing to play favorites—an interesting and in this case effective strategy.

Throughout the coverage of the Seafirst incident, the reporters aggressively pursued the story and had the support of the editors. The editors at the *Times* allowed reporters almost complete freedom, encouraging neither more nor less intensive coverage. The only complaint *Times* reporter Heberlein had was that he felt that occasionally a headline or pull quote was misleading. The *PI* is the "second" newspaper in Seattle and often sees itself as playing catch-up with the *Times*. The editors at the *PI* frequently encouraged their reporters—Pam Leven primarily, but others as well—to get more from the story than they thought was there. According to Leven, "The editors treated it like a murder investigation. They were always seeking new clues." In general, she noted, the editors at the *PI* had a very low opinion of banks and bank executives. This view probably influenced the editors' evaluation of events. The editors probably also felt the competition with the *Times* and hoped for a scoop that would boost the paper's reputation and help sell newspapers. This kind of competitive pressure would less likely be felt by editors at the *Times*.

In general, the reporters were satisfied with the way Seafirst dealt with them. The public relations staff was always available and was frequently called at home when questions arose. The public relations people were sensitive to deadlines, understood what kind of information was needed, and made senior bank executives available when possible; and senior management, with the advice of the public relations staff, appeared relatively open and forthright. In general, very little friction or animosity developed between the press and Seafirst. The press did not always get all the information it wanted, but it was generally convinced that Seafirst was divulging all the information it felt it could.

OPEN PRESS RELATIONS: THE BEST ALTERNATIVE

Press relations at Seafirst were open throughout the crisis. The case represents a classic example of how being open with the press can be successful. The Seafirst experience is the kind that many public relations executives and journalists will point to as an example of enlightened media strategy. The question remains, however, as to the extent that the Seafirst case can serve as a general guide for business-media relations.

The crisis was one in which Seafirst was culpable. The headlines in the *PI* put it succinctly: "The Wrecking of Seafirst. A handful of executives bring down the bank." Although mitigating circumstances can be found—Seafirst executives were not alone in their belief that oil prices would move forever upward, and many of the loans made would not have gone bad had oil prices not fallen when they had—it is a fact that a few executives committed the bank to a lending strategy that failed. This was the primary fact with which public relations had to deal. In this kind of situation, every unexplained "no comment" will automatically lead the press to conclude that an attempt is being made to hide damaging information.

Seafirst also had a large number of investors, shareholders, and customers who were concerned about its financial condition. These people would inevitably get much of their information from the news; thus, it was imperative that Seafirst's views be presented. The only way to assure this was for Seafirst to talk to the press.

At the beginning of the crisis a conscious decision was made to be open with the press. The two immediate press contacts in the corporate communications office—Katie Weiss and Art Merrick—were professionals with a philosophical disposition to be open with the press. Randy James had no formal training in public relations but also agreed that an open press strategy was best. Throughout the crisis the three—particularly James and Merrick—influenced managerial decisions in the direction of openness.

The issue was such that news could not be suppressed. There were numerous independent sources of information about Seafirst, from information disclosed with the collapse of Penn Square to an informant who worked in Seafirst's energy department. In many instances, Seafirst did not disclose information to the press but responded to information the press already had. The refusal to respond would guarantee only that the bank's position would not be considered.

The crisis resulted in a permanent increase in the importance of the public relations function. Although prior to the crisis James reported directly to the president, the situation reinforced the importance of the function to management. The perceived success in handling the crisis assured that organizationally and functionally public relations would play a larger role in managerial decision making.

By and large the media covered the story accurately and with a minimum of speculation and sensationalism. A number of the reporters I spoke with were quite concerned that they not be responsible for causing a "run" on the bank. The reporters, in fact, seemed most concerned about the responsibility exhibited by their own editors and headline writers.

The best coverage of the crisis was by the two Seattle papers. These reporters were most informed about the issue and the circumstances surrounding it, and it showed in their stories. The reporters who came in from out of town for a two- or three-day stay typically had the most inaccurate coverage.

The press reacted to Seafirst's press strategy favorably and felt that there was a serious attempt to be open and forthcoming with information. Weiss and Merrick in particular were highly regarded by the media.

Several lessons can be gained from the Seafirst experience.

First, in a crisis such as Seafirst experienced, relative openness with the press is probably the only practical press strategy. With stories breaking constantly and independent sources of information widely available, something significantly less than full disclosure will invite speculation, suspicion, and result in more negative stories than would otherwise occur. The problem is to convince management that this is the case. The natural response is to not admit mistakes by issuing a "no comment" and hoping the press will go on to something else. This can be an effective strategy in certain situations, as will be seen in the case of Beckman Instruments, but not in the kind of crisis that Seafirst faced.

Second, the public relations function tends to become isolated from management because it is not considered relevant to mainstream business operations. In a crisis, however, it becomes central to managerial strategy. Then the issue becomes how much the public relations staff knows about the business. Merrick commented that, in retrospect, he thought he could have responded more effectively to questions posed by the press if he had known more about the energy lending business. He felt that periodic and fairly intensive briefings by key executives would have helped. James, on the other hand, felt that as head of the department he had access to such information. The press, however, generally felt more comfortable dealing with Merrick than James, pointing to the need for all public relations professionals to be more informed of business operations.

Third, the Seafirst case also illustrates the need for senior management to monitor the public relations function. As we have seen, the ideology of public relations practitioners tends to fall between that of senior management and the press; and because of their educational background and current function, public relations practitioners tend to identify with the press to a much greater extent than managers. As the anecdote about Weiss makes clear, management must make sure that the public relations practitioner's primary loyalty is to the interests of the company and not to providing reporters or the public with information.

Fourth, generally speaking, the better informed the reporter, the better the news coverage. This is exemplified by the superior coverage of the two Seattle newspapers, where the reporters were most familiar with the case.

Finally, biased and sensational reporting does not always emanate from the reporter. Editors have an important role. Writing headlines, rewriting leads, changing or adding adjectives to create "zest," and the selective use of pull quotes can be misleading. Editors also can pressure reporters to find stories and report issues that will attract readers or viewers. All of this can lead to distortion above and beyond that which the reporter writes.

In general, however, the press can be "managed," as the Seafirst case illustrates. The significant fact to consider is that the press strategy developed is consistent with the situation. No overall prescription, such as "always be open with the press," is adequate for every situation and every company. However, with the correct strategy business can communicate its message to the public by dealing effectively with the press.

8

Closing the Door on the Press: The Beckman Strategy

THE KIDNAPPING

Beckman Instruments, Inc., a Southern California-based company that manufactures scientific instruments, found itself at the center of media attention when two of its employees were kidnapped by terrorists in El Salvador. The kidnapping and the circumstances surrounding the release of the hostages were potentially front-page stories. Beckman's strategy, however, reduced the actual coverage to an absolute minimum. Here is how it happened.

On September 21, 1979, the State Department notified senior executives at Beckman Instruments that two of its employees— Dennis A. McDonald, manager of Beckman's subsidiary in El Salvador, and Fausto R. Bucheli, an engineer from one of the company's Fullerton divisions—had been kidnapped and the driver of their car killed. Senior management, including the CEO, chief legal counsel, and the heads of public relations and personnel, among others, met the next day. This group, minus the CEO, formed a special crisis management task force that met daily until the hostages were released. Almost immediately upon learning the news, Beckman contacted Fred Raynes, a security consultant first retained by the company nearly two years before. Raynes immediately flew to El Salvador where he served as the chief negotiator for the release of the hostages.

The initial press contact with Beckman occurred that same Friday evening. By the next day a senior Beckman executive had contacted at least one reporter with information about the incident. Shortly thereafter, under the direction of the special task force, the first of three press releases was drafted and made available to the press. No news conference was held at that time. Only two news conferences were held during the entire episode: one after the political advertisements the terrorists required Beckman to place had appeared and another after the hostages were returned. The two other news releases were issued after the ads were placed and the hostages returned; throughout the crisis the only contacts with the press were by telephone, on a daily basis during the first few weeks.

The terrorists, who were claiming to represent the Revolutionary Party of Central American Workers, had two demands. The first was that Beckman place a full-page political advertisement in selected newspapers in the United States, Europe, and Latin America. The ad had to be translated—the copy supplied was in Spanish—and the publishers of the various newspapers contacted. The time line was short, and management felt the pressure. The publishers of most of the newspapers were cooperative, but in a few instances the ads simply could not be placed. The concern was that if all of the ads were not placed, the lives of the hostages would be jeopardized. As it turned out, the ads the company was able to place satisfied the terrorists. The second demand was that Beckman pay a ransom of a substantial but still undisclosed amount.

After the ransom was paid, the hostages were released and flown to Ontario International Airport in Southern California, where they arrived Thursday night, November 7, 1979, following forty-seven days of captivity. That same evening—as soon as the chartered plane carrying the released hostages entered U.S. air space—the press was notified by Beckman that there would be a press conference the next morning.

At the November 8 conference the third news release was issued and senior management was on hand to answer questions. The Beckman employees taken hostage were not at the conference and were never made available to the press.

PRESS STRATEGY: NO NEWS IS GOOD NEWS

If one can imagine a spectrum between open press relations and closed press relations, Beckman would fall at the closed end of that spectrum. There are a number of reasons why Beckman chose to employ such a policy and a number of reasons why it could be employed.

One reason is that Beckman's products, scientific instruments, are sold to other institutions—businesses, universities, government agencies—rather than to individuals. Thus, while the company has a relatively high profile in the city of Fullerton, where it is head-quartered and where most of its operations and employees are located, the nature of its products makes it unknown to large numbers of consumers. Such a company normally will not have the kind of public visibility that a company which provides a product or service to individual consumers will have. In addition, Beckman enjoyed a favorable local reputation because, as a large and successful company, it was a highly visible economic asset to the community. The combination of low public visibility and favorable local reputation both encouraged and made possible a relatively closed relation with the press.

There is another reason why Beckman developed a closed approach to the press. As a company that makes scientific instruments, a large proportion of its employees are scientists and engineers. The typical scientist or engineer is not flamboyant and does not seek high public visibility. This is not to say that no engineer or scientist is flamboyant or publicity oriented, but that most tend to be more low-profile, conservative, and technically oriented. To a large extent, the culture of an organization can be explained by the type of employee recruited to the firm. A retailing firm will attract, on average, a different personality than an accounting firm. These personalities collectively influence organizational culture. This is the case with Beckman. The company developed a relatively closed or conservative approach to the press because that was the approach that was most consistent with its organizational culture. This was reflected even in the public relations staff. Both Bill Gregory, the public relations manager, and Elke Eastman, his assistant, agreed that the company's approach to press relations was conservative and both thought the strategy appropriate and successful (see Exhibit 8.1).

In accordance with this relatively closed and conservative press philosophy, all communications with the press about the kidnapping were strictly controlled by the Beckman crisis management task force that was formed at the outset. The task force met each morning to review events and decide upon company strategy—including press strategy. Bill Gregory was looked upon to provide guidance on what the press should and should not be told. What the press could be told each day was determined by the task force, and a "news line" was developed and distributed to the public relations staff to be given to reporters in response to questions. Press contact was tightly controlled; there were no impromptu press conferences or comments.

The immediate rationale for this strict control was to ensure the safe return of the hostages and to protect the well-being of their families. Thus, very little information about the situation, other than comments such as "the captives are safe" and "we have been in touch with the kidnappers," was disclosed.

The rationale for this strictly controlled press strategy was two-fold. First, there was a concern that too much information could be dangerous. In particular, if wrong or misleading information were to be made public, the ongoing negotiations could be jeopardized and the lives of the hostages endangered. (As was later discovered, this was a legitimate concern. Bill Gregory made a comment to Kim Murphy, a reporter for the *Orange County Register*, indicating that some of the newspapers in which the terrorists had directed Beckman to place ads would not accept them. The resulting story in the *Register* implied that Beckman was not going to meet the terrorist's demands. The terrorists read the story—perhaps they had a clipping service—and confronted one of the hostages with the alternative: death. After his release, one of the former hostages said to Gregory, "So you're the guy that almost got me killed!") Thus, Beckman's strategy to reduce the likelihood that wrong or misleading information would be reported in the press was to severely limit the amount of information shared with the press and to strictly control its content.

A second reason for maintaining a closed press strategy in this incident was ideological. The company did not want to aid and abet the terrorists in their revolutionary cause. The company was forced to provide the terrorists with free publicity by placing the ads and to give them a financial base by paying a substantial ransom, but it did not want to provide additional, unintended publicity. Thus, the press was given as little information as possible.

PRESS REACTION: RELUCTANT ACCEPTANCE

The first time Elke Eastman heard about the kidnapping was when she received a call at home on Friday evening, September 21, 1979, from Kim Murphy, a reporter from the *Orange County Register*. Murphy had seen a report on the news wire about the kidnapping in El Salvador of two Beckman executives. Eastman knew nothing—not even how the reporter got her home phone number. (The press contacts in many public relations departments routinely provide reporters with their home address and phone number.) Eastman told the reporter that she would try to get some information and that she would call her back. Eastman then unsuccessfully attempted to reach Bill Gregory at home. She then called Dr. Arnold Beckman, the company chairman. Beckman confirmed that he had received a call from the State Department indicating that the kidnapping had occurred. Eastman emphasized the need to make some sort of a statement to the press. Beckman referred her to Robert J. Steinmeyer, vice-president-legal, who had been given responsibility for the matter. Eastman contacted Steinmeyer and informed him about the inquiry from the press. He agreed to talk to the reporter. When Murphy called a second time later that same night, Eastman called Steinmeyer and he contacted Murphy. At this time, only the barest details about the kidnapping were released. (The second press release is reproduced in Exhibit 8.1, the third in Exhibit 8.2.)

The next morning the crisis management task force first met and considered the situation. It was decided not to release the names of the hostages until contacts had been established with the families. After the families were notified—and in the presence of intense pressure from the press—the first of only two news releases was issued. The release identified the hostages, the terrorists, and the demand to place the political advertisements coupled with the threat that the hostages would be killed if Beckman did not comply. The names and phone numbers of the reporters were taken with the promise that they would be contacted if and when more news developed. The reporters were contacted periodically and told what had been agreed upon at the daily task force meeting.

The result was that the press got very little information and almost nothing that the task force did not approve. However,

Exhibit 8.1

Second Beckman Press Release

The text of the second of three press releases. This release was issued as the demand by the terrorists that advertisements be placed in newspapers around the world was met. The first press release confirmed the kidnapping of McDonald and Bucheli.

October 10, 1979

To ensure the safe return of its two employees now being held by the Revolutionary Party of Central American Workers (PRTC), Beckman is complying with PRTC demands that it place advertisements containing a PRTC Revolutionary proclamation in a number of newspapers, specified by the PRTC, in Central America, the U.S. and Europe.

The company expects the safe return of its employees after the advertisements have appeared.

The Beckman employees, Dennis A. McDonald, 37, and Fausto Busheli, 41, were kidnapped by the PRTC last Sept. 21, in San Salvador, in an attack in which the Americans' Salvadoran bodyguard, José Luis Paz Tratara, was shot to death. The PRTC says the Americans are well.

McDonald is manager of APLAR, a Beckman subsidiary in El Salvador which makes parts for electronic components. Bucheli, an engineer based by Beckman's Fullerton, Calif., headquarters plant, was in San Salvador on a business trip.

APLAR employs some 500 Salvadorans. It has been in operation for about two years.

The PRTC advertisement claims responsibility for the "capture" of the Beckman employees, denounces "North American Imperalists," and urges support of the PRTC revolutionary cause.

Beckman's principal reason for silence—the overriding concern for the safety of the hostages—apparently was convincing enough to enlist media cooperation. The number of stories that appeared locally was limited, and what did appear was accurate. There was little sensationalism and speculation. Beckman was pleased with the coverage.

Events also conspired to reduce media attention on the incident. The two local papers, the *Los Angeles Times* and the *Orange*

Exhibit 8.2
Third Beckman Press Release

The text of the third of three releases. Throughout the entire episode there were only three press releases and three news conferences.

November 7, 1979

Dennis A. McDonald and Fausto R. Bucheli, the two Beckman Instruments, Inc., employees kidnapped in San Salvador Sept. 21, returned safely (early this morning) and are now with their families. Both men appear to be in good condition.

They will be given thorough medical examinations and then spend time resting and relaxing with their wives and children at an undisclosed location.

McDonald, 37, is manager of APLAR, a Beckman subsidiary in San Salvador which manufactures electronic components. Bucheli, 41, an engineer in Beckman's Heliport Division, Fullerton, Calif., was on a business assignment at APLAR.

The men were freed (last night) after the company met demands of the kidnappers, the Revolutionary Party of Central American Workers (PRTC). The demands included the publishing of a PRTC revolutionary proclamation in newspapers in the United States, Central and South America and Europe, and a substantial amount of money.

County Register, surprisingly did not pursue the issue with particular vigor. This appeared to be more the result of a lack of interest and attention on the part of the papers' editors than the reporters. At the time of the kidnapping, there had been a high turnover of editors at the *Times*, and the editor of the *Register* simply did not give the story high priority. Kim Murphy, the *Register* reporter who broke the story, called the whole affair "frustrating." Not enough information from Beckman and not enough support from her editor were the causes. Because the story contained few events that could be depicted visually—the press never even had the opportunity to photograph the freed hostages much less to interview them—television coverage was minimal.

Since the negotiations were secret, the only source of information was Beckman, and the press strategy employed by Beckman effectively controlled the flow of information. Finally, the Iranian hostage crisis effectively diverted press and public attention from Beckman.

The reaction of the press to the closed press strategy of Beckman thus was unusually compliant. The concern about not endangering the lives of the hostages during the delicate negotiations explained and rationalized the limited information provided by Beckman. None of the local reporters, who normally would be expected to give the incident the most intense coverage, were given the necessary support by their editors, and once the Iranian hostage crisis occurred, the newsworthiness of the Beckman story diminished.

When the hostages were finally released, the press conference conducted by Beckman the next day satisfied reporters in the short run. The reporters' desire to interview the former hostages was countered by Beckman's request that they be given time to adjust to their ordeal and to reunite with their families. As soon as the hostages returned, Beckman advised them on their right to privacy and against talking to the press. One employee readily agreed; the other was more ambivalent. Beckman's response was that once the employee talked to the press the company would no longer serve as intermediary and he would be on his own. The ambivalent employee chose not to talk to the press.

Some six months after the release of the hostages, and at a time when the press again began pressing for interviews, Beckman made a decision to close the issue. The press was told that nothing further would be gained by discussing the issue and that as far as Beckman was concerned the case was closed. The issue was not pursued further until several years later when Kim Murphy contacted Bill Gregory and asked to do a postscript. She was denied. In conversation with Murphy some six years after the event, she told me she still cannot understand why Beckman would not allow the employees to be interviewed or why the company was so secretive about the incident even after the employees were out of danger. The press, or at least Murphy, remains frustrated, but little can be done without the cooperation of Beckman. Besides, who really cares six months much less six years after the fact?

Simply put, the Beckman strategy worked.

IS THE BECKMAN EXPERIENCE TRANSFERABLE?

The Beckman strategy worked in the situation described. Indeed,

Photograph 8.1
Kidnap Victim Returns

Kidnapped Beckman employee Dennis A. McDonald upon his arrival at Ontario International Airport. The kidnapped employees never met with the press. (Photo courtesy Bill Gregory)

NEWS BUREAU
BECKMAN INSTRUMENTS, INC.
2500 Harbor Boulevard
Fullerton, California, 92634

CONTACT: Bill Gregory (Ext. 1045)

HOMECOMING—Dennis A. McDonald, 37, (left) one of two employees of Beckman Instruments, Inc., held captive by revolutionary group in El Salvador since Sept. 21, exults at Ontario, Calif. airport. at 1:30 a.m. today (Thurs., Nov. 8). Beckman engineer Fausto R. Bucheli, 41, the second hostage, returned with McDonald. Robert J. Steinmeyer (center), vice-president-legal for Fullerton-based firm and Leslie W. Chapin (right), group vice president, are among Beckman executives who welcomed McDonald and Bucheli.

it may have been the best strategy to employ for that company in that situation. How universally applicable is the closed press strategy employed by Beckman?

In the opinion of the Beckman public relations staff involved in the incident, the overall strategy employed was unassailable. They felt that Beckman controlled information effectively and that what appeared in the press was generally accurate and responsible. The public relations manager was very influential in developing media policy during the crisis and was quite satisfied with its outcome. When asked whether in retrospect they would have done anything differently, the only comment other than "no" was by Bill Gregory. Gregory commented that his only misgiving was that he wished he could have explained to the press why he could not give them more information. However, since this additional information might have been reported and might have endangered the hostages, he had concluded it was a risk he and the company were not willing to take. Misgivings, perhaps, but no change in strategy.

The Beckman strategy was successful because of many characteristics unique to the company and to the incident. An understanding of those unique characteristics will engender a better understanding of when a closed press strategy is viable and when it is not. Those characteristics, some of which have already been discussed, will be summarized.

1. The type of company affected the range of press strategies available. As a manufacturer of scientific instruments, Beckman did not have the responsibility of answering to a large number of consumers. There was no concern, as there might be with a consumer products or service company, with consumer confidence. Disclosing little information to the press—even with the possibility of press speculation—would have a negligible affect on business, at least in the short run.

2. The type of corporate culture affected the strategy chosen. A large proportion of Beckman management was scientists and engineers, who typically are relatively conservative and cautious regarding media strategy. The company's past media strategy was to disclose what was necessary but not to seek publicity. This strategy was effective in that Beckman had relatively little to gain from such publicity. This may be contrasted with a company such as McDonald's, where public goodwill generated through favorable

publicity can increase sales just as unfavorable publicity can decrease sales. Thus, Beckman's primary concern was to communicate information about company operations to investors and employees, and the press was considered a way to augment that communications effort.

3. The fact that Beckman was perceived as the victim made a closed press strategy more workable. Beckman was thrust into a crisis situation through no apparent fault of its own. Beckman had been doing business in a country where there was considerable political unrest and instability. However, in assuming the risks of such involvement, Beckman also tried to minimize danger to its employees by hiring an antiterrorist consultant some two years before the kidnapping. Beckman had taken appropriate precautions and could not be accused of negligence. The fact that Beckman was the victim made press inquiries less critical and allowed the company to be much less responsive to those inquiries than would otherwise be the case.

4. As Beckman officials emphasized, excessive press coverage could have endangered the negotiations and the lives of the captives. The negotiations that were ongoing throughout the crisis served as a rationale, reluctantly accepted by the press, for not disclosing information. Another argument used by the company, probably less persuasive to the press, was the desire not to give the terrorists "free" publicity.

5. Events allowed Beckman to minimize press coverage even after the hostages were released. The day after the release, Beckman held a second press conference and issued its third and last news release. Reporters were never allowed to interview the hostages, and the only pictures of them obtained by the media were released by Beckman. The initial rationale for not allowing the interviews was to allow the hostages to adjust to their ordeal and to reunite with their families. When it became clear that the company was never going to allow the interview time, other events had overtaken the crisis. Beckman had nothing to gain by the additional publicity and, perhaps, something to lose if either of the employees was at all critical of how the incident was handled. Because Beckman was not a consumer products company which would be sensitive to public opinion, it could withstand considerable press pressure. Ironically, however, very little press pressure was applied.

At first this was because the Iranian hostage crisis occurred, and then because time reduced the newsworthiness of the issue.

6. The press responded to the Beckman strategy with what is best described as uneasy frustration. When the story broke, it was considered big news by the reporters involved. This was the second time that employees from a major American company had been taken hostage: Would it become a trend? If the companies could be relied upon to pay a substantial ransom in this kind of instance, would kidnappings become more frequent? Is it safe for Americans to do business in foreign countries? In the long run can the U.S. government allow companies to pay these ransoms? What are the foreign policy implications of the kidnappings? These are the issues of which important news stories are made, but Beckman refused to be drawn into speculation for what seemed to the press at the time plausible reasons. Still, the underlying fact was that very little information was forthcoming. Had the Iranian hostage crisis not occurred when it did, or had it been resolved before the Beckman crisis, the press undoubtedly would have applied much greater pressure on the company for information.

CONCLUDING COMMENT

To say that a company must be open with the press is belied by the Beckman example. Beckman was cooperative but not open with the press. It was, in fact, about as closed as can be imagined given the circumstances. In reviewing the case I could not find any reasons other than what Beckman executives told me to account for the company's silence. There was no pressure from the government, the employees were not also employed by the CIA, the company had nothing to hide in its handling of the crisis. The apparent bottom line is that company executives—including those in the public relations department—simply were not interested in publicity in general and could not see how the company could benefit by it in this particular instance.

There are two important lessons to be learned in this case. The first is that in the right circumstances information can be withheld from the press with no adverse consequences. The press will not like it, but it can be done. The second is that withholding information requires careful thought. As the Beckman case illustrates, there were a wide variety of factors that contributed to the success of Beckman's strategy. Had any one of those factors been absent, the strategy would very likely have failed.

9

Crisis Communications
and Toxic Waste: The Case of
BKK Corporation

THE ONGOING CRISIS

BKK Corporation owns a 583-acre plot of land in West Covina, California. In 1962, the West Covina City Council issued Home Savings and Loan Association, which at the time held title to the land, a Class II land use permit allowing solid waste disposal on the site. BKK leased the land from Home Savings and Loan in 1963. In 1969, BKK applied for and received a Class I license, which allowed it to dispose of hazardous waste on 140 acres of the land. In 1978, BKK purchased the 583 acres from Home Savings.

Prior to 1978, the land immediately adjacent to the landfill was vacant, and the site itself, including its acceptance of hazardous waste, generated little controversy. BKK maintained a low public profile. During the period, however, the purpose of the landfill had changed. When the original Class II license was granted, the agreement was that when the ravine was filled with refuse, it would be covered with dirt and turned into a park. By being granted a Class I permit, the life of the landfill was extended and park plans postponed. In return, BKK and the city agreed to impose a 10 percent tax on the landfill's gross receipts.

In 1978, things began to change. A home building boom hit West Covina. W & A Builders, Inc., constructed homes immediately adjacent to the site, and other builders constructed homes on vacant land somewhat further away. The site was no longer isolated. Why the city allowed homes to be built so close to the landfill, and what exactly the builders told buyers about the landfill and the current plans for it, rapidly became a moot point. The homeowners adjacent to the site quickly became concerned about the smell and the potential health hazards from the toxic waste. They complained to both BKK and the city council. BKK rsponded by initiating steps to control the odor.

Toward the latter part of 1980, the Palos Verdes, California, hazardous waste dumpsite was closed. This left BKK as the only state-certified hazardous waste disposal site in Southern California. Thus, BKK inherited all of the Palos Verdes hazardous waste business (which was very lucrative) as well as all of the toxic waste concern (which was very intense). The media began to focus on BKK not only because of the intensity of community concern but because it had now become the only operating hazardous waste site in Southern California. Each and every complaint was now documented and reported. Stories about noxious odors emanating from the landfill, tanker traffic, toxic spills, potential health hazards, and the like, appeared in the local media almost daily. BKK was, according to then Vice-President Ken Kazarian, in a position of "damned if we do and damned if we don't."

On Monday, February 9, 1981, the city council ordered the planning commission to begin hearings on the revocation, suspension, or amendment of BKK's unclassified land use permit.

On Tuesday, April 28, 1981, a public nuisance petition was filed against BKK in the West Covina city clerk's office. The petition stated, in part:

We the undersigned, residents of West Covina and surrounding areas, out of concern for the health, safety, and comfort of our community, do declare BKK Landfill Corporation to be a public nuisance, and call for the West Covina City Council to revoke the unclassified use permit of the BKK Landfill Corporation and permanently close down all dumpings of any materials, liquid or solid, toxic or nontoxic, at the aforementioned site.

Although no action was taken at the time, the petition was the precursor of an initiative that would be filed with the city that summer. Ken Kazarian, now president, said this of the issue: "It was a matter of survival for us at the time. There were a group of people out there who were trying to put us out of business. BKK just responded." BKK responded by entering the political arena and by attempting to use the media to influence public opinion.

In the summer of 1981, the Coalition of West Covina Home-owners' Associations prepared an initiative which would prohibit hazardous waste from being disposed of at the landfill. The proposition was submitted to the West Covina City Council, which placed it on the November 1981 ballot without recommendation. BKK and Proposition K, as the initiative was known, became the hottest political issue in the city.

The passage of Proposition K would have been disastrous for BKK. The company's political consultant and strategist, Lynn Wessell, went to work and managed to get an initiative, called Proposition L, also placed on the ballot. Proposition L, which would take effect only if Proposition K passed, would have raised the taxes of all West Covina residents by $1 million annually to make up for the revenue lost from BKK. The $1 million revenue loss, BKK pointed out, represented 7.3 percent of the city's revenue. Ultimately, Proposition K was defeated. (Wessell, incidentally, wrote the argument against Proposition K and the arguments for and against Proposition L that appeared on the ballot.) This was a remarkable accomplishment for BKK. Early polls had indicated that 60 percent of the registered voters supported Proposition K. BKK's campaign efforts can be credited with its defeat. This short-run victory did not eliminate future problems, however.

In July, 1981, SB 501 was passed by the state legislature and signed by the governor remanding authority over BKK and its operations to the state. BKK's involvement in the passage of SB 501 was controversial, and BKK was accused of excessive and sometimes unethical attempts to influence local, state, and federal elections. BKK executives readily admitted to campaign contributions and intense lobbying activities.

In October, 1981, California Governor Jerry Brown issued an executive order mandating alternative hazardous waste disposal. The order gave the incentives needed for BKK to build the first modern, offsite treatment facility for liquid hazardous waste near San Diego.

Early in 1982, the Coalition of West Covina Homeowners' Associations initiated a recall movement aimed at several members of the city council who had supported BKK (see Exhibit 9.1). Again, BKK entered the local political arena. Through the West Covina Good Government Committee, BKK spent in excess of $30,000 opposing the recall. The recall drives were defeated, but BKK was strongly criticized for its participation.

In January, 1983, BKK opened the first modern offsite treatment facility for liquid hazardous wastes in California. At a cost of $2.5 million, the treatment facility represented a substantial commitment of resources and, it was hoped, a new, less controversial future for BKK.

In June, 1983, BKK announced the grand opening of the new treatment center to the press. Press response to the announcement was anemic and little coverage resulted.

At 5:00 P.M. Tuesday, July 17, 1984, an event occurred that would lead ultimately to the closure of BKK for hazardous waste disposal. Twenty-one families living near the landfill were evacuated when high levels of methane gas were reported around their homes. The incident received extensive media coverage, with many stories implying a connection between the gas and the hazardous waste disposal. (There was no connection. Methane gas is produced by the decomposition of organic matter—the nontoxic waste also disposed of at the site.)

Various state and local agencies converged on BKK. The City of West Covina initiated legal action in Los Angeles Superior Court. To BKK's relief, the court imposed order on the sometimes conflicting demands of the regulators, and a new gas collection and monitoring system was completed. Some five months later the evacuated families also filed a lawsuit against BKK, but settled out of court by the end of 1986.

By the end of 1984, BKK had closed its offsite treatment center, which had proved uneconomical. Although the facility no longer accepted hazardous waste, it continued to operate as a transfer station.

In November, 1985, BKK reached an agreement with the West Covina City Council to cease landfill operations by 1995.

PRESS STRATEGY

BKK's press strategy evolved, in response to public pressure, from nonexistent to aggressive. As the strategy evolved, BKK not

Exhibit 9.1
Recall Mailer

A mailer opposing the recall of two West Covina city councilmen. The recall was actively opposed by BKK.

Your Vote Counts More than Ever, Tues., Mar. 23.

The Recall leaders have maintained a surprising low profile during the closing weeks before their big election opportunity Tuesday.

They had hoped it would remain a dark secret that they have filed claims totalling $50 million against the City of West Covina ... which means against every property owner in town. The secret is out.

Proposition 13 has provided for special assessment districts to deal with the treasury emergency that would occur if a future City Council awarded all or any part of the $50 million to the small group of claimants. A $50 million shortage, for example would require a special assessment average of $2,174 against each of West Covina's 22,996 local property owners. Half of that large settlement would average $1,087 each. And so on.

It would be much better to make sure that City Council is never handpicked by the Recall leaders and their cash-demanding friends. It will take your vote to accomplish that.

MEASURES SUBMITTED TO VOTE OF VOTERS / MEDIDAS SOMETIDAS AL VOTO DE LOS VOTANTES		
Shall Robert Bacon be recalled (removed) from office of City Councilmember?	¿Deberá Robert Bacon ser destituido (depuesto) de su cargo como miembro del Concejo Municipal?	YES (SI)
		NO X
Shall Kenneth I. Chappell be recalled (removed) from office of City Councilmember?	¿Deberá Kenneth I. Chappell ser destituido (depuesto) de su cargo como miembro del Concejo Municipal?	YES (SI)
		NO X
Shall Chester Shearer be recalled (removed) from office of City Councilmember?	¿Deberá Chester Shearer ser destituido (depuesto) de su cargo como miembro del Concejo Municipal?	YES (SI)
		NO X
Shall Herb Tice be recalled (removed) from the office of City Councilmember?	¿Deberá Herb Tice ser destituido (depuesto) de su cargo como miembro del Concejo Municipal?	YES (SI)
		NO X

YOU MUST
VOTE NO
4 TIMES!

Go to the polls. Vote NO on the Recall. 4 Times.

only developed an open relationship with the press, when Ken Kazarian, first as vice-president and later as president, became its
principal spokesman, but actively attempted to influence public
opinion by other means.

The strategy to influence public opinion was developed in 1979
when BKK hired Lynn Wessell as a public relations consultant and
political strategist. Wessell's approach was to actively support West
Covina City Council members and candidates friendly to BKK and
to oppose its political opponents. The attempt was to isolate the
opponents of the landfill by portraying them as irrational and
sometimes fanatical citizens who had the misfortune to live next to
the landfill. The fact was that not all West Covina residents were
equally affected by the landfill, and the most concerned citizens,
not surprisingly, tended to be those in closest proximity. It was rea-
soned that if the other West Covina residents could be persuaded
that the landfill did not pose a significant threat to the health and
safety of its neighbors, and if they could be convinced further that
BKK provided a significant benefit to the city, the opponents could
be isolated.

Another strategy devised by Wessell for BKK was to publish its
own newspaper, the *West Covina Chronicle* (see Exhibit 9.2). The
Chronicle has a circulation of 40,000 and cost $100,000 annually to
publish. BKK's name was prominent on the masthead. The
Chronicle carried news about the community, emphasizing that
BKK was a part of the community and a good citizen. When BKK
awarded scholarships to outstanding students, they were featured
prominently in the *Chronicle*. Favorable news stories were published on West Covina city councilmen who supported BKK, and
although many issues carried positive stories about BKK which by
implication refuted its critics, some carried nothing about the company. The overall message—that BKK was part of the solution and
not the problem and that its opponents were not entirely rational—was subtly but effectively presented. The *Chronicle*
avoided the image of a PR piece for BKK to the extent that the
editors of competing weeklies became greatly concerned about its
existence. One survey indicated that the *Chronicle* was more
popular than many of the local papers.

As Ken Kazarian (see Photograph 9.1) assumed responsibility as
principal media spokesman for BKK, he developed a strategy of

Exhibit 9.2
West Covina Chronicle

The front page of the *West Covina Chronicle*, published bimonthly between 1980 and 1984. The *Chronicle* included news about the community along with good news stories about the BKK landfill.

Eutek Tells City: 'Odor Risk' Here to Drop 95% Under Expanded Controls

West Covina Chronicle

| MAIL EDITION | FRIDAY, OCTOBER 23, 1981 | 50,000 READERS |

Medfly Find Here Assures Spraying Until Christmas

National Award Given Dr. Day

Historical Feature

West Covina's first swimming pool was this Weir box, whose gates regulated the flow of irrigation water or filled the dam for 1813 cool-offs in icy well water. The Maxson family shows how it was done at N.W. corner of Sunset and Merced. See City's history, Page 3.

After their cool-off in the Weir box, the Maxson children walk home on Sunset Ave. Today, Queen of the Valley Hospital occupies site on the left of photo.

Photograph 9.1
Ken Kazarian, BKK President

As BKK Corporation president and principal media spokesman, Kazarian adhered to a policy of open press relations.

being open with the press. Kazarian had no formal media training, but was personable and voluble and developed a good relationship with the press. His philosophy was to "talk until they [reporters] said they had to get off the phone." The reporters generally appreciated his openness, and he was able to get BKK's side of the story in the press most effectively. Kazarian's message was essentially the same as that devised by Wessell: explain BKK's position on the issue fully and imply that its opponents did not have accurate information.

BKK did not use written press releases or hold press conferences, but it had a policy of getting its message out and defending its interests whenever possible. BKK always had representatives at public hearings concerning it, even if it was not formally asked to appear. The press came to BKK, and BKK was accessible, but it did not seek out the press—with one exception. The exception was the opening of its offsite hazardous waste treatment facility. The press was invited to the grand opening, and press releases announcing the event were sent out. The result was almost no press coverage. A "good news" story just doesn't have much appeal (see Exhibit 9.3).

An interesting aspect of BKK's press strategy was that the press felt that it had no strategy. As a consequence, Kazarian was able to develop a greater rapport with the press than would have been the case otherwise.

MEDIA VIEWS

Almost without exception, the media approved of BKK's press relations. Kazarian, or someone equally knowledgeable, was invariably available when the press wanted information or an interview. In discussing media relations with Kazarian it was obvious that he enjoyed dealing with reporters and liked being in the news.

Exhibit 9.3
BKK Press Release

Partial text of one of the few press releases issued by BKK. The attempt was to get a "good news" story about the opening of the company's liquid hazardous waste treatment facility. Very little press coverage resulted.

May 20, 1983

An historic advance in the disposal of hazardous liquid waste was marked today in the official dedication of the BKK Corporation's new $2.5 million AP-TEC II neutralization and reduction plant in Chula Vista, south of San Diego.

The "state-of-the-art" plant will be able to treat and render harmless about 90% of the types of liquid wastes—acids, alkali, and oils—now being created in San Diego County, Kenneth B. Kazarian, Jr., president of BKK, told reporters.

He explained that 70% of the bulk—and sometimes more—of the waste stream is water. The AP-TEC II plant will remove and treat the water into a sewerable quality. The clear water will then be disposed of in a sewer.

Several Los Angeles-area journalists who had covered BKK were interviewed to get their opinion on the effectiveness of BKK's press strategy. In the course of the interviews, it became apparent that Kazarian was the focal point for the media, and few of the journalists knew about Wessell's role or had had contact with him.

Deborah Hastings, a staff reporter for the *Los Angeles Times*, had covered BKK since the gas leak and residential evacuation in July, 1984. Except during the hectic days of the evacuation, Hastings found Kazarian easy to contact and very open and honest. When Kazarian was not available or when legal questions arose, Hastings was referred to the company attorney.

Hastings, who at the time of our interview was doing a profile on Kazarian, had very little negative to say about the way he dealt with the press. In Hastings's view, this is in part due to the fact that "he has always felt that I have treated him fairly. I know there have been times when he wouldn't talk to other reporters, but I could get through to him."

In Hastings's opinion, Kazarian always appeared to be the decision maker, and she found quotes from him useful. Stories about BKK that have run in the *L.A. Times*, she explained, "almost always have quotes right from the president himself." This access to the top benefits BKK, according to Hastings, because "What you basically put in your story is their [the homeowner's] version and BKK's version and try to run right down the middle."

BKK was criticized in the press for the allegedly heavyhanded tactics used to defeat Proposition K and to support its political allies. Hastings spoke with approval about the way Kazarian responded to the critics. Kazarian's position was that BKK had a right to defend itself in the political arena, and if that meant contributing to the campaigns of friendly politicians, that was what it would do. Hastings commented in this regard, "They don't pull any punches in admitting, yes, they did contribute a lot of dollars." Although many people opposed this kind of participation, Hastings added, "You have to admire his honesty."

Dan Medina, an investigative reporter for Los Angeles-based KHJ News, was somewhat less complimentary about Kazarian's approach to the media. In April, 1984, Medina attempted to contact Kazarian to do a story on BKK. Initially he had a difficult time getting in contact with Kazarian. When he finally made contact and requested an interview, Kazarian asked him to submit questions in writing. Medina informed him that that would be impossible. Medina commented on the interview: "He was a likable fellow once I finally got a chance to meet him. He also tried—like everyone—to push the positive in what they were doing in the plant [offsite treatment center] down in San Diego. He provided a video of it which we used."

Medina's approach on the feature was to look at the story from the point of view of BKK—Kazarian's perspective—as well as from the point of view, as Medina put it, of "the people who live around it and who say it stinks." Medina said he was pleased with the way the feature turned out and felt that it was accurate. (Kazarian was not so pleased. Apparently, at one point Medina stated that BKK would no longer accept hazardous waste, when in fact it would. The result, according to Kazarian, was an immediate 20 percent loss of business.)

Jim Foy, editorial director for KNBC News in Los Angeles, had done a story on BKK but had no direct contact with Kazarian. Members of his news staff, however, did have contact and reported that he was very cooperative.

Foy had some interesting and relevant comments on press strategy. From his point of view, press releases are not very effective. "Nobody reads them," he commented. He thought the best way to deal with an ongoing crisis such as BKK faced is by letter. Keep the media informed, and let them know whom to contact, he advised. The contact should be someone who is knowledgeable and in a position of authority, not the PR director. On general press strategy Foy commented, "BKK should position itself as more concerned than the most staunch environmentalist" about public health and safety. On BKK's failure to get significant media coverage of its offsite treatment facility, Foy noted, "BKK won't get any positive press. Very few companies get positive press. [It's] because of the nature of the news [media]. They'll get positive press in the trade publications, but the news media tend to focus on things that are going wrong—not the things that are going right."

Given Foy's advice, BKK's press strategy is on track. Its principal spokesman is the company president, few press releases are issued, but it is accessible to the press, and the company's interests are aggressively represented.

Warren Olney, a reporter and political editor for KCBS News in Los Angeles, first covered BKK in 1979. Olney had a very positive opinion of BKK's press strategy in general and Ken Kazarian in particular. Olney commented on Kazarian's style: "Very friendly, very cooperative. He has been willing to answer any questions that I wanted to put to him." He was also quite willing, said Olney, to let camera crews onsite to take pictures.

Olney had high praise for BKK's effectiveness. "I think overall, considering that they started out being perceived as real villains by a lot of people—certainly the homeowners and I think a lot of reporters as well—they did pretty well." His only criticism of Kazarian was that sometimes he seemed to overwhelm the interviewer with information and his perception that Kazarian may sometimes be perceived as "a little too slick and fast talking."

In covering BKK, Olney never relied solely on company sources but always sought other points of view. BKK's strategy of openness and Kazarian's execution of it allowed the company's position to be presented effectively.

Ron Curran, a staff reporter for the *Los Angeles Weekly*, covered BKK in an article entitled, "The Real Menace of BKK." Curran, who said he spent a month researching the article, was satisfied with the information supplied by BKK. He commented that Kazarian was "very cooperative. He always returned my calls promptly." Curran did not think BKK had a press strategy, only that it was open and accessible. Curran felt that Kazarian was pleasant to deal with and that he answered questions fully.

The interview with Curran was interesting in another respect. Curran's article was probably the most negative and inaccurate of any of the stories about BKK. When Curran was asked about possible bias, he responded, "It is in the nature of the paper to take a position." However, he seemed genuinely surprised to learn that Kazarian did not like the piece and remained convinced of its accuracy. In the article's defense, Curran noted that it had won the California Newspaper Publishers Association award for the best feature story in a weekly newspaper. Press awards do not always reward accuracy.

In general, the journalists who had covered BKK had a positive impression of its media relations. This is remarkable, given the enormous amount of negative press the company received. President Ken Kazarian is largely responsible for the press's positive impression. He seems to have been able to combine effectively a policy of openness, honesty, and aggressive defense of BKK's interests that favorably meets the expectations of the press.

CONCLUSION: MAKING THE BEST OF AN IMPOSSIBLE SITUATION

In retrospect, the closure of the BKK landfill in West Covina was probably inevitable. Increasing public concern about "toxic waste" since the Love Canal incident makes the existence of a hazardous waste disposal site in the middle of a major residential area a political impossibility.

Still, BKK's media strategy must be considered a success in that it prolonged the economic life of the landfill by at least five years. Had the methane gas leak and subsequent evacuation not occurred, BKK may have been able to accept hazardous waste for several more years, but even a perfect press strategy could only postpone the inevitable.

Despite the comments to the contrary by several journalists, BKK did (and does) have a press strategy. The strategy may not have been as explicitly devised by Kazarian as it was by Wessell, but the strategy was operative nonetheless.

The overall strategy was one of openness to the press. An overriding concern of both Wessell and Kazarian was to get BKK's message to the public. Contacts with the press were always welcome, and BKK even went so far as to publish its own newspaper. The general policy of openness was complemented by the personality and interests of the company president. Kazarian genuinely seems to enjoy talking to the press and obviously gets satisfaction out of the publicity he and his company receive.

However, openness is not the totality of the strategy. To the press, Kazarian appears simply to be answering questions as forthrightly as possible and explaining BKK's position, and perhaps, subjectively, that is all he thinks he is doing. The message, however, bears the stamp of the strategy devised by Wessell to defeat Proposition K in 1981. That strategy is to aggressively defend BKK's interests by minimizing the risk the landfill poses to the health and safety of the community—and the studies conducted so far support the claim that the risks are minimal—and to portray opponents, often only by implication, as hysterical and irrational. The message, effectively delivered, portrays BKK as a responsible company providing an important public service for which it receives nothing but criticism.

This strategy has been effective in winning elections, influencing legislators, and in dealing with the press. Given the unrelenting criticism, BKK could have easily developed a more accommodative and less successful strategy. If BKK had conceded points to the opposition, it could very well have strengthened the opposition's position by inputing a certain legitimacy to its arguments. In my initial interview with Kazarian, I made a comment about the "explosive" levels of methane gas that led to the evacuation. His immediate response was to explain that explosive levels of gas were never found, which was true, and to add, "Those people didn't have to be evacuated. Everyone just overreacted." On opponents of the landfill: "Most of the complaints were coming from disgruntled homeowners concerned about a decision they alone made. They were looking for someone to blame."

In sum, BKK's press strategy was a remarkable success. In the end, however, events simply overwhelmed it.

10

Financial Writing Awards: A Business-Media Symbiosis

SOLVING A NAME RECOGNITION PROBLEM

The cases discussed in the book so far have dealt with how a firm manages the media when the firm has attracted media attention. Seafirst had huge loan losses and had to respond to an insistent press. Beckman Instruments responded to press inquiries about the kidnapping of two of its executives. BKK Corporation found itself in the middle of a toxic waste controversy and was forced to defend its position in the press. In each of these cases the company was reacting to press inquiry, and rather than positive publicity being the primary goal, the object was to avoid negative publicity.

There is also the possibility of using the media to enhance a company's image. The most common way of doing this is through the medium of advertising. If a company becomes associated with fine products or services, its public image will be enhanced. Some companies also have resorted to image advertising, where the attributes of the firm are discussed without direct reference to its products or services. The idea is that if the image of the firm is enhanced, consumers will demand more of its products or services.

However, there are problems with advertising. It is expensive and better suited to promoting a product or service than an image. Image advertising has been criticized as being vague and the results difficult to measure. In addition, in many instances advertising may not be considered appropriate. Some firms eschew advertising altogether. Even though now allowed to do so, many doctors, lawyers, and accountants do not engage in advertising, for example, because they do not think it is appropriate to the dignified image they wish to maintain. This leaves the news media as a means of promoting a company's image. The object of most press releases is at least partially to enhance the firm's image, but as anyone who has dealt with the press is aware, it is very difficult to get journalists interested in stories that reflect favorably on the organization. This is in part because journalists are understandably reluctant to give free publicity. It is also, to put the matter bluntly, because good news does not seem as interesting as bad news to journalists. Thus, press releases are of limited value in promoting a company's image.

There are other ways that the media can be used to enhance a company's image. Pannell Kerr Forster (PKF), a large public accounting firm with a name recognition problem, embarked upon an interesting strategy. The accounting firm is the fourteenth largest in the United States, with more than 300 offices worldwide. While the "Big Eight" accounting firms have widely recognized names and are considered the elite of the big accounting firms, they also have a relatively fixed market share. Serving mostly the largest industrial and nonindustrial companies, a Big Eight firm typically will grow at the expense of another. PKF, on the other hand, serves medium- and smaller-sized companies and nonprofit organizations and has experienced a rapidly growing customer base. Still, its name and status are not widely known. The benefits of an enhanced public image would be an even greater customer base and, equally important, a greater opportunity to hire the best accounting graduates.

Although improving PKF's public image was considered a top priority, advertising was not considered to be compatible with the image the firm was trying to project, and normal press contacts obviously were unsuitable for this objective. The firm's managing partner, Charles Kaiser, discussed the image problem with Ed Welch, of Cunningham & Walsh, a public relations firm on retainer for PKF. The idea they agreed upon was to sponsor some sort of competition. One thought was an art contest, where artists around the country would be invited to submit their works. They finally decided to sponsor a financial writers contest.

This idea had appeal in part because Charles Kaiser had an interest in good writing and was distressed at the quality of writing among the public generally and accountants particularly. The idea of a contest that would feature good financial writing thus had considerable inherent appeal to him. The program goals as officially stated in *Panorama*, a quarterly magazine published by PKF, are as follows:

Our goals for the Achievement Awards Program were, first, to encourage and recognize superior contributions by practicing journalists in interpreting complex financial issues and in creating a better public understanding of those issues, and, second, to let our professionals, and the accounting profession as a whole, know that we must write clearly and concisely, we must write to be understood.

The overriding reason for sponsoring the program, however, was that it was considered an appropriate way by which PKF could increase its name recognition and enhance its public image. By focusing the competition on financial writing, PKF could target the people it wanted most to reach: financially oriented business executives and the business press.

ORGANIZING THE AWARDS PROGRAM

In 1984, a program to honor excellence in financial reporting was inaugurated by PKF. Although the contest was sponsored by PKF, the details—such as judging, publicity arrangements, attracting contestants, and the like—were developed and administered in conjunction with Cunningham & Walsh (see Exhibit 10.1).

From the beginning, it was recognized that the success of the competition would depend upon the perceived integrity of the judging process. This process was two-tiered. The first tier was the initial screening committee made up of five members of the New York Financial Writers Association. The screening committee was composed of journalists, including representatives from the *New York Times*, *Newsweek*, and *U.S. News and World Report*, among others.

After making its determination, the screening committee was to submit the finalists to a panel of three judges. The judges consisted of a journalist (Chris Wells, administrator of the Baghot Fellow-

Exhibit 10.1
Achievement Awards Brochure

Pannell Kerr Forster
announces the
1985
Achievement Awards
Program for
Outstanding
Financial Writing

Brochure announcing Achievement Awards Program and calling for entries. Brochure was mailed to major newspapers and business publications across the country. The brochure also listed the 1984 winners.

In 1984, the first year of the competition, there were 80 entries; in 1985 there were 125. The 1986 competition will also include an award for broadcast journalism.

Courtesy Pannell Kerr Forster.

ship in the Graduate School of Journalism at Columbia University and now a senior editor at *Business Week*), an academic (John C. Burton, dean of the Graduate School of Business at Columbia University), and a business leader (Donald P. Kelly, chairman of Beatrice, Inc.).

The winner of the award would receive $3,000 and a sculpture, and five other journalists would receive honorable mentions and $1,500. The awards were presented at a luncheon hosted by PKF, and the winning articles were reprinted in PKF's *Panorama*.

The articles were judged on how effectively they had "created a better public understanding of a complex financial issue."

MANAGEMENT'S VIEW: COMPLETE SUCCESS

The competition has now been conducted for two years, and a third is planned; but how successful has the competition been? Is it worth the considerable cost? Let us attempt to answer these questions first from the point of view of PKF.

In quantitative terms the program seems to have been a success. Entries were solicited throughout the year from newspapers and magazines across the country. Brochures and letters explaining the competition and urging submissions were sent to editors. Eighty entries were received in 1984, the first year of the competition, and 125 in 1985. In both years, about 1,500 invitations to the luncheon were sent out. The first year about 60 people attended the luncheon, the second year about 170. (The competition was held in New York in 1984 and Los Angeles in 1985.) In the 1985 competition, members of the broadcast media expressed interest. In 1986, a special broadcast category will be created and an award given for outstanding broadcast journalism.

Results of the competition are widely distributed; some 40,000 copies of *Panorama* (see Exhibit 10.2) are printed and distributed, and the luncheon takes place in a different part of the country each year.

The cost of the program is substantial. For the Los Angeles luncheon, including awards and speaker, it was estimated to be about $70,000. This does not include the time spent on the affair by the public relations firm—estimated to be about a month—or the indirect cost of the program committee—estimated by the chair-

Exhibit 10.2
Panorama

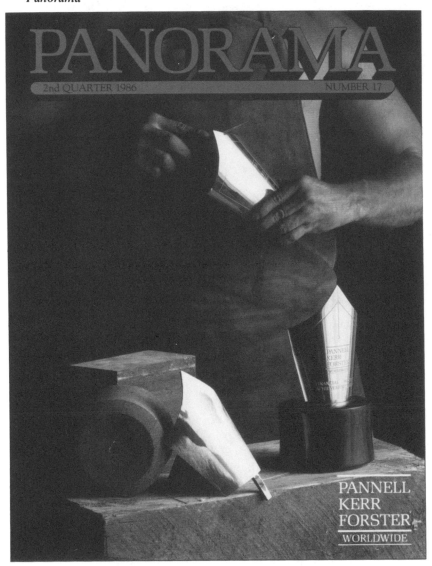

Courtesy Pannell Kerr Forster.

man, Michael Cohn, to be about 200 hours for each of the three members.

Members of PKF and its public relations firm with whom I spoke were unanimous in their agreement that the competition was indeed a success.

Managing partner Charles Kaiser was enthusiastic about the program, noting how it had expanded in the second year. When asked about how effectively the competition enhanced PKF's name recognition and image, he responded rhetorically: "Did you know who we were before the luncheon? Do you know now?"

Michael Cohn, the 1985 program chairman, also thought the competition was a success. Cohn noted that there was no preestablished budget for the program and added that if people thought it successful no one would complain about the cost. There were no complaints. Almost everyone involved, he said, thought the competition was a huge success.

Ed Welch, the account supervisor with Cunningham & Walsh who had worked on the program since its inception, also felt it was successful. In his opinion, the competition "catapulted" the name of Pannell Kerr Forster into prominence. He also felt the journalists thought highly of the competition and that it raised the media's awareness of the firm.

Kathy Rubinger, PKF director of communications, was equally enthusiastic about the competition. She thought that in addition to better public recognition, the competition vastly increased media awareness of the firm. It was also a way she could become more familiar with the media and make media contacts. She felt that the competition already had increased media awareness of PKF and would result in more journalists calling PKF for information and more often getting PKF's name in the news.

In sum, there was enthusiastic support for the program by those involved, with a variety of benefits cited. Interestingly, however, there has been no attempt to formally measure the success of the program. No survey has been conducted or contemplated to determine if PKF name recognition has increased. No one even has contacted the journalists involved in the competition to assess their opinion.

The reader should find the opinion of journalists interesting.

JOURNALISTS' VIEW: WARY ACCEPTANCE

Several journalists who received awards were questioned on the following topics: (1) their opinion of PKF's reason for sponsoring the competition; (2) their opinion of the integrity of the selection process; (3) the importance of the award to them and to their colleagues; and (4) the likelihood that the competition will in fact improve business reporting.

Carol J. Loomis won the Financial Writing Achievement Award (first place) for her article, "The War between the Gettys," published in *Fortune*. Loomis was a member of *Fortune*'s board of editors and has covered a wide range of business topics since joining the magazine's staff in 1954. In 1980, she served as one of six panelists in a nationally televised presidential debate. Loomis received her bachelor's degree in journalism from the University of Missouri and has won more than a dozen awards for outstanding business and financial writing.

Loomis felt that PKF started the awards program for the publicity value but also from the sincere belief that "there's virtue in good financial writing." She did not feel that anyone had tried to influence her views of PKF, stating that "there is no reason to doubt the integrity of the motive."

When asked about the selection process, she laughed and said, "I'd be the last person to question that!" She went on to add, however, that she was familiar with most of the judges involved and felt that they represented the best in journalism, higher education, and business.

Loomis said that she felt that receiving the award would be personally and professionally beneficial to any journalist and ranked the PKF award with other nationally recognized awards—such as the Lobe, Tuck, and John Hancock awards—as important and serious.

Loomis added, however, that she doubted the ability of any award to improve financial reporting. "For instance, I didn't sit down to write 'The War between the Gettys' with the idea in mind that I was going to try to win an award with it. I just wrote what I thought was a good story and was lucky enough to be noticed."

Jerry Roberts, a reporter for the *San Francisco Chronicle*, received an honorable mention in the 1985 competition for an article written with Daniel Rosenheim, Erik Ingram, and Diane Curtis, entitled "The Legacy of Proposition 13." A graduate of Harvard University, Roberts joined the *Chronicle* in 1977, where he covered city hall, the state capital, and a number of political campaigns before becoming assistant city editor for politics, law, and government in 1982. In 1985, he was named investigative editor.

Roberts felt that PKF was motivated by a desire for name recognition and had established the awards competition for that purpose. He did not feel, however, that PKF expected anything of him personally.

Roberts was not familiar with the details of the judging process, and when asked what the award meant to him, he replied, "It's sure nice to get the money!" He then added, "It's also nice to be recognized, but awards from colleagues are always nicer." He said that receipt of the award was a surprise to him. The *Chronicle* has a staff person who submits articles on behalf of the newspaper for such competition and that person had apparently submitted the article.

Roberts noted that there seems to be a general trend by newspapers to attempt to win awards and that management is very "award conscious" in its assignment and editing. Thus, he concludes that the availability of awards does make for better reporting. He also noted that he has seen an increasing emphasis on business reporting in the last few years.

Daniel Rosenheim was a coauthor with Jerry Roberts on "The Legacy of Proposition 13." In 1985, Rosenheim joined the *San Francisco Chronicle* as economics editor. Prior to that he had been a business reporter at the *Chicago Tribune* and earlier worked at the *Chicago Sun-Times* as a business reporter and special writer. Rosenheim was graduated from Wesleyan University in 1971.

"Clearly, PKF hopes to gain free publicity," Rosenheim said in the interview. "I met one of their PR people at the luncheon," he added "and he admitted as much to me." Rosenheim was the most skeptical of the winners interviewed and felt that he could never view Pannell Kerr Forster with impartiality again. He is concerned about the potential conflict of interest, or at least its appearance, by an award program sponsored by a for-profit organization. He emphasized that he would never feel comfortable contacting or being contacted by PKF. When asked about the integrity of the judges and the selection process, he stated emphatically that he had never been put in a compromising position by anyone involved, and although he was not familiar with the details of the selection process he had no reason to doubt its professionalism.

He mentioned an example of a potential conflict of interest in which he almost recommended PKF to one of the companies he was interviewing for a story. Somewhat chagrined, he added, "Nothing like that would have happened if they hadn't given me an award." However, he did appreciate receiving the award. "It's very nice."

When asked about the ability of awards programs to increase the quality of business reporting, Rosenheim responded, "The existence of awards is a motivational force for some reporters. You'd hope it wouldn't be, but it is because awards help us professionally." To the extent that reporters write to receive awards, he concluded, they do have influence.

Richard Ringer, a reporter for the *American Banker*, received an honorable mention in 1984 for an article he wrote with Bart Fraust entitled "Linked Financing." Ringer received his bachelor's degree in sociology from the College of Steubenville and attended the Graduate School of Journalism at Marquette University. Ringer also had been a freelance writer and a reporter for the *Chicago Tribune* and *Milwaukee Journal*.

Initially, when asked about PKF's motivation for the award, Ringer laughed. When the question was repeated he said that he had no reason to believe that their motive was not to promote good financial writing.

He had high praise for the integrity of the judging process and said that the judges were well selected. Alluding to the previous question about motivation, Ringer said, "PKF can put on the contest for any reason they choose. The judges are really what make the thing legitimate. In this competition," he added, "the judges were beyond reproach."

Ringer said he liked receiving the recognition but added that he did not write to receive awards. He noted that his editor submitted the article for him. Asked about how others reacted to the award, he said, "Everybody patted me on the back in 1984, but this is 1986. What have I done this year?"

Ringer does not believe that awards can improve the quality of business writing because journalists do not write to receive awards.

"You can't let the prospect of awards influence your behavior."

Bart Fraust received an honorable mention in the 1984 competition for the article he wrote with Richard Ringer. A graduate of Queens College of the City University of New York, he worked as a copy editor for the *American Banker* for six years before becoming a reporter.

When asked why PKF would sponsor such an award, Fraust said he had often asked himself the same question. He did not see how PKF could benefit. "I suppose their primary motivation was to gain publicity," he commented, "but I don't really think they got any."

Fraust was not familiar with the details of the selection process but knew the names of the judges and thought they were of high caliber.

The award, however, did not have much meaning for him, and he was somewhat confused by receiving it. "I'd never heard of them and didn't quite know what to make of them giving me $1,500 that I hadn't even asked for."

Fraust has been the recipient of several other writing awards, but they all had been awarded by press clubs and had not involved money. Like many of the other journalists interviewed, Fraust felt that awards by peers are more prestigious than those given by a private company, no matter how much money is involved. "This Pannell Kerr Forster thing sort of fell out of the sky, and who knows why they're doing it," he said. "When you receive an award from your peers, you know you've really accomplished something."

Fraust did not think journalists wrote to receive awards, especially from companies, and he did not think that offering such awards would have any influence on the quality of business writing.

ACHIEVEMENT AWARDS: A GOOD START

A careful evaluation leads to the conclusion that the PKF Financial Writing Achievement Awards Program is off to a good start. If continued, the firm's image and name recognition is likely to be improved, and there is a good argument that it will actually improve business journalism. Whether the program is cost effective compared to other methods of enhancing image and name recognition is open to question and will not be dealt with here. That the competition is innovative and effectively administered, however, has been clearly established.

What has the awards competition actually achieved to date and what is it likely to achieve in the long run? One thing that should be noted at the outset is that there is a fundamental ambivalence in the purpose of the program. The ambivalence involves promoting PKF's image on the one hand and establishing an award that will have the respect of journalists on the other. PKF need not disassociate its name from the competition entirely—although many journalists no doubt would prefer that it did—but it must emphasize more than it has the integrity of the selection process. Journalists resent being part of an awards process where the real purpose is to celebrate the sponsor. This was an objection to the contest raised by Daniel Rosenheim. His objections are probably a bit extreme, and it is unlikely that most journalists would begrudge PKF some recognition for its sponsorship. The point to remember is that the publicity benefits must be subtly and tastefully achieved.

When all is said and done, the recognition journalists covet most is from their peers. It is frequently not recognized how profoundly journalists—especially print journalists—are oriented toward their peers rather than the public. Journalists may consider themselves public servants, but they judge the quality of their service not according to its public estimation but according to its peer estimation. If a journalist's colleagues think an article is good, it scarcely matters what the public and sometimes even the editors think Hence, the critical element in establishing the legitimacy of the PKF competition is peer review. As has been seen, the program was devised with a substantial element of peer review: the screening committee is composed entirely of practicing journalists, and one of the three judges is a journalist. Nevertheless, several of the awardees were not familiar with the selection process. To establish the credibility of the competition in the opinion of journalists, the peer review element in the selection process must be publicized more extensively. As *Chicago Tribune* business editor Jim Squires noted in an interview, numerous organizations offer awards, but only a few other than those offered by the profession itself have any legitmacy in the eyes of journalists or their editors. The key, Squires noted, is whether the intent of the award is to promote excellence in journalism or to promote a special interest. The best way to demonstrate that the purpose is excellence in journalism is to have a strong element of peer review.

In addition to the peer review process, another way to enhance the value of the award is to associate it with a neutral organization such as a university. The Champion-Tuck Awards are administered by the Tuck School of Management at Dartmouth College. PKF's public relations firm indicated to me that they also are considering such an affiliation, which would enhance the credibility of the award but would probably diminish its public relations value for PKF. (The Champion-Tuck Awards are sponsored by Champion but are known simply as the Tuck Awards. Squires of the *Tribune* thought that one of the positive attributes of that award was that the sponsor was more or less anonymous.)

Another way by which the stature of the awards could be enhanced would be if the awards were presented to the winners at the luncheon by a prominent journalist rather than by PKF executives. Again, this would somewhat diminish the public relations value of the award to PKF but would enhance its value to the journalists.

There is no question that the PKF Financial Writing Achievement Awards can become as legitimate and well regarded as, say, the Tuck Awards. All that needs to be done is to maintain the legitimacy of the judging process by carefully selecting the panel of judges and the screening committee, associating the judging process with a neutral third party such as a university, and modifying the awards ceremony somewhat. A good start already has been made.

The final question that remains to be discussed is what, if any, influence such an award can have on business reporting. The potential, I believe, is greater than most journalists like to think, but less than most business executives would hope.

Regardless of what journalists say about not writing for awards, the fact is that more awards are given and received in journalism than any other group short of actors. Given the popularity of awards, it would be strange if they were not important to journalists. Awards are popular and important to journalists because they do not get much response from the public, other than an occasional letter to the editor here and there. Everyone needs recognition, so journalists give it to themselves.

In fact, the better journalists do write for awards, in the sense that they aspire to write something their peers will consider good enough to single out for acclaim. The problem is that journalists identify the good story with the unusual and the sensational; in most instances, that is to say, with bad news. Bruce Ramsey, a business reporter at the *Seattle PI*, noted that the only award he ever received for business reporting was for an investigative piece he did on the near collapse of Seattle-First National Bank.

Unlike the professional awards, the PKF competition can establish its own criteria for excellence, and as long as the criteria are legitimate—and those established by PKF clearly are—"good news" stories can be rewarded. I would be surprised if there are not many business journalists who share Ramsey's frustration for not being recognized for what they consider good business reporting: explaining and interpreting complicated business and economic issues to the public. An award with criteria such as PKF's can give public recognition to such stories, and it can provide moral support and incentive to journalists who wish to write them. The only reservation I would have is that the criteria established by PKF do not explicitly enough encourage the selection of "good news" stories.

11

Open and Closed Press
Strategies: Review and Comment

THE CASES IN REVIEW

As the press strategies discussed in this section indicate, there is no one best press strategy. Different strategies are appropriate to different situations and different companies. The best way to manage the media is not to be totally open or totally closed, or even partially open or closed, but to have a clear idea of what is to be accomplished and analyze the situation to determine what strategy will work best.

Seattle-First National Bank had established a policy of open press relations prior to its crisis. Art Merrick, head of corporate communications, and Katie Weiss, who worked with him, were public relations professionals philosophically committed to open press relations. Randy James, who was in charge of corporate affairs, although not trained in public relations, also was committed to open press relations.

The crisis itself was one in which Seafirst was culpable. Seafirst's participation in questionable energy loans precipitated the crisis. Ultimately, the survival of the bank was in question. The press had access to a variety of news sources, from unnamed informants in the bank itself to federal regulators. The press had enough independent information to publish stories without Seafirst's participation. In addition, Seafirst needed to reassure its customers and the community that it was facing the crisis responsibly and that the money of its depositors was safe.

In the Seafirst case, the philosophy of openness was consistent with the exigencies of the situation. Seafirst's relatively cordial relationship with the local media and its philosophy of openness enabled it to communicate its message to the public effectively.

An inadvertent benefit of the crisis was to more closely integrate the public relations function into the corporate decision-making process. This integration resulted initially from the importance of public relations during the crisis but was continued when Richard Cooley became chairman. To a degree unusual among senior executives, Cooley believed in the importance of public and media relations. Integrating public relations into the managerial decision-making process promises long-term benefit to the organization.

Beckman Instruments had a closed press relations strategy. The company was not consumer oriented and had nothing to gain from a high public profile. With an organizational culture dominated by scientists and engineers, the company actually tended to avoid publicity. The public relations staff reflected the view that the press should be held at arms length and the company kept out of the news.

Unlike Seafirst, Beckman was not responsible for its crisis. There were no outside sources of information about the incident available to the press, and the press was dependent entirely upon Beckman to supply information, of which it supplied very little. Only three press releases were issued during the crisis—the first acknowledging the kidnapping, the second announcing that the ads demanded by the terrorists were being placed, and the third that the hostages had been returned safely. The press never was allowed to interview the kidnapped employees.

The rationale for disclosing so little information initially was that the safety of the hostages required it and after their release that they needed time to adjust to their ordeal and reunite with their families. The press was frustrated by the Beckman strategy but accepted it reluctantly.

The Beckman case illustrates that a company need not always disclose everything, but it should also be clear that a closed press strategy is effective only in rather restricted situations. Too often, if employed, such a strategy generates press hostility.

The third case study was of the ongoing crises at the BKK landfill. Like Seafirst, BKK also pursued an open press strategy. Unlike Seafirst, BKK did not simply respond to the press but actively attempted to influence press and public opinion.

BKK's overall strategy consisted of three points: be open with the press and respond fully to all press inquiries; minimize the risk of the landfill to public health and safety and to assure that the company was doing everything possible to keep these risks minimal; and portray opponents of the landfill as irrational and extreme and, hence, irresponsible.

The BKK strategy also worked. Indeed, although events ultimately overwhelmed it, given the severity and multiplicity of the crises, the strategy can be described as an enormous success.

In each of these cases the strategies employed were successful because each was appropriate to the situation. The remainder of the chapter will focus on some general observations concerning the proper press strategy.

OPEN AND CLOSED PRESS STRATEGIES

In the short run, press strategies deal with two basic components: the content of the message and the amount of information disclosed. The concluding chapter in Part I included some suggestions on how a message can be framed so that it will be presented to the public by the media with minimal distortion. BKK was effective in shaping the content of its message in such a way as to establish itself as a competently managed and concerned company frequently criticized by not entirely rational community groups. The approach was effective not only in causing the press to dismiss these critics but also in forcing the press to take BKK's position seriously and featuring it prominently in stories. Not much more can be expected. What will be discussed in the remainder of this chapter, however, is the amount of information it is appropriate to disclose.

When to Talk to the Press

An obvious rule of thumb is to communicate with the press when silence is likely to be harmful. When, for the second time, cyanide was found in Tylenol capsules, Johnson and Johnson announced at a press conference that, in view of tragic recent events, it had decided to discontinue manufacture of the capsule. The message was clear and one that Johnson and Johnson felt needed to be communicated to restore public confidence in the company and the tablets it would continue to market. For Johnson and Johnson not to have been open with the press immediately upon reaching its decision would have been extremely damaging. A similar situation applied to Seattle-First National Bank when it was disclosed that it had participated in questionable loans with Penn Square. It was imperative that Seafirst communicate with the press in an attempt to shore up the confidence of its depositors and the public.

It is important to be open when the press already has one side of the story. In a controversial and emotionally charged situation such as BKK found itself, it was imperative that the press be provided a reasonable response to the critics' charges. The press had ready access to BKK's opponents, who made highly exaggerated charges about the hazards associated with the disposal site. Knowing that the critics' views would be presented in any case, it was imperative that BKK present its side. This, of course, does not guarantee a balanced story, but it does at least provide the opportunity for an alternative view that would not otherwise appear.

To the press, objectivity often means balance, in the sense that if there are three parties to a controversy the views of each are presented. For a company not to express its views in such a situation—even if it believes that its opponents charges should not be dignified by a response—is to have its side go unreported or, what may be worse, to allow the press to speculate on why the company chose not to respond.

It is also important to communicate with the media when the message will result in good press. The problem is that good press is difficult to get. Journalists typically are not interested in "good news" stories. When BKK opened its new, nonpolluting $3.5 million hazardous waste treatment facility, the press was not interested. The press has more interest in reporting toxic waste accidents than their prevention. Despite the fact that "good news" stories are seldom used, it is important to communicate them to the press, if only to help establish a favorable image of the company with the journalist, an image that may be beneficial the next time a "bad news" story erupts.

How a "good news" story is presented can affect its newsworthiness, however. An insightful interview with a senior executive of a major firm is inherently more newsworthy than a press release. In addition, if in the interview some "human interest" comments are included—"I agonized over the decision to lay off 10 of our em-

ployees'' or ''Even after making the decision to invest $3 million in
the project, we weren't sure it was the right one''—the interview becomes even more newsworthy. How good news is presented is of
critical importance.

When Not to Talk to the Press

There are times when it is advisable not to communicate with the
press. While the decision to not talk to the press needs to be carefully considered, in general, this strategy is not as dangerous or
futile as the press would like to have companies believe. Journalists
typically assert that when a company does not present its side of an
issue the press has no choice but to present only the other side.
Often, however, a story is effective only when two views are presented, and sometimes the company is the story and without its
comments there is no story. An example was the case of an aircraft
retrofitting company that had serious financial problems but was
anticipating a major new contract that would provide the company
with the financial cushion needed to solve them. A reporter wanted
to do a story on the problems the company was having, but company officials feared that a negative story would damage business.
The company declined to participate. No story was published. Absent company comment, there was no story.

Another instance when information need not be divulged to the
press is when it has no other source of information. This was the
situation in which Beckman Instruments found itself. The press
knew about the kidnapping but little else. Since Beckman controlled the information, without its participation there was no
story. To the extent that a company has a monopoly of information
and can control its dissemination, it can choose a policy of not talking to the press with relative impunity.

Finally, the press will accept a ''no comment'' response if there
seems to be a compelling reason for it. Beckman had a compelling
reason—the safety of its employees. Reasons for not talking to the
press, however, must be genuinely compelling. Journalists have a
vested interest in disclosing information, and mere inconvenience
will not seem compelling. The best rationale is that innocent parties
will be harmed needlessly in some important way.

A caveat is in order about not talking to the press. The primary problem with this strategy is that it generates resentment among journalists. In addition, when a company chooses a strategy of not being open with the press as did Beckman, it risks alienating the most sympathetic journalists—the business reporter who covers the company on a continuing basis. Pam Leven, formerly a business reporter for the *Seattle PI*, recalled how one company she covered invariably refused to comment on its press releases. When she called to ask about a particular release announcing unexpectedly high profits, she was told the company policy was to not comment on the releases and so they could not, as she requested, "explain" why the profits were high. Leven reported in her news story that in an interview a company spokesman said they could not "explain" the unexpectedly high profits. The quote was accurate but, of course, deliberately out of context. It is important to maintain good relations with the press, and to do this there must be some appreciation for the job of the reporter.

The final case discussed in this book—the Pannell Kerr Forster Financial Writing Achievement Awards—did not involve crisis communications. The immediate purpose of the awards was to generate name recognition for PKF. That they were able to use the media for this purpose was unique. More important than the immediate purpose of the award, however, is its long-term consequence: to improve business reporting. The next chapter will examine this and other long-term strategies that business can employ to improve business-media relations.

12

Managing the Media: Concluding Comments and Observations

CAN THE MEDIA BE MANAGED?

Most public relations professionals would deny that they attempt to manage the media and most journalists that they can be managed. In reality, however, the media can be managed—in the sense that by understanding their biases, motivations, and needs, business can more effectively communicate its message to the public through the media. The mass media of communication constitute a means through which reality is selected, organized, interpreted, and presented to the public. In this process there is inevitably a certain amount of distortion. The distortion is not random but predictable. Business needs to understand this process of distortion and effectively counteract it—this is the essence of media management.

Some advice on how to manage the media was offered in Chapters 6 and 10. This advice suggested how to deal with the media on a daily basis and in crisis situations. What has not been discussed is how the media affects public opinion and what business can do encourage a more favorable media and public opinion climate.

HOW THE MEDIA INFLUENCE PUBLIC OPINION

As was argued in Chapters 1 and 2 and illustrated in the case of journalists in Chapter 3, the politics of the new class (which includes journalists) is predominantly liberal and antibusiness. This is evident in business-news reporting. Business and business executives are seen as powerful and somewhat sinister forces in society that must be watched carefully by the press and regulated closely by government if they are not to subvert the public interest. It is not that journalists are opposed to private enterprise or that they believe all business executives are evil, but that there is an underlying hostility and suspicion reserved especially for business.

The origins of the new class are structural—a consequence of our high-technology, information-oriented society. The antibusiness ideology of the new class results from the fact that it sees itself in competition with business for power and influence. The new class is not monolithic, however: There are conservative intellectuals and journalists. This small but extremely important group of intellectuals and journalists provides business with an opportunity to influence the ideological composition of the new class.

Public Opinion Formation

Public opinion formation is a very complicated process. Social scientists do not know exactly how public opinion is formed, and I do not presume to present a complete explanation here. The rudiments of opinion formation are fairly obvious, however, and sufficient for the purposes of the present discussion.

The basis of public opinion formation is the personal experience of individuals. Our firmest judgments about the world come from our direct experience in it, but experience includes more than direct experience. It also includes what other people tell us about the world. These others include spouse, coworker, journalist, teacher, and the like, and are what social scientists sometimes refer to as "opinion leaders." Opinion leaders help individuals explain and interpret reality. The influence of opinion leaders is greatest where the individual has little or no direct experience of reality.

An example of where opinion leaders may be influential is a discussion of economic policy. Journalists may be of the opinion that President Reagan's "supply side" policies help the rich and hurt the poor. As objective as the journalist may attempt to be, his view of Reagan's policies *will* influence the way he reports them. The average person does not have enough knowledge of economics to form an independent opinion. He looks to opinion leaders for explanation and interpretation.

Although individuals react to opinion leaders in terms of their own personal situations—their income, political party affiliation, whether they identify with rich or poor, and the like—in the short run opinion leaders can be influential. Journalists are opinion leaders, and their collective reaction can influence public opinion. Journalists can prejudice public opinion on an issue but they cannot change opinion. Ultimately, the opinion of journalists will be tested by experience. If an individual is told by the media that Reagan's economic policies will help only the rich, he may presume this to be true in the short run. Over time he will begin to note how he and his friends are faring under the policy and how it compares to the economic policies of the past. If the individual finds himself worse off, the view of the journalists will be confirmed. If he finds himself better off, it will be discounted.

A similar logic applies to people's attitudes toward business in general. Americans traditionally have been suspicious of large concentrations of power. Business, particularly "big" business, appears to be such a large power concentration. This underlying public suspicion of business is reinforced by journalists who are even more suspicious than the public. Because most people do not have direct experience with big business, they tend to be influenced by the views presented in the media. Thus, the media probably create more public hostility and suspicion of business than would otherwise exist.

Generally, it is true that the less direct, personal experience the public has with an issue, the more influential the media will be in influencing public opinion. Thus, the influence of the media on public opinion is important and in the short run may be decisive, but in the long run people make decisions based on fairly concrete personal experience that is not influenced significantly by the media.

If personal experience ultimately prevails, what effect do the media have on public opinion?

As mentioned previously, the media influence opinion most on issues that are remote from personal experience. In business and economic issues particularly, the influence of the media in the short run is enhanced because the media do not reflect the full diversity of American public opinion. The liberal, antibusiness bias of the media will tend to push public opinion in that direction. If the media included more diversity of opinion, if it more accurately reflected the entire spectrum of public opinion, its influence on public opinion in the short run would be less.

There is another way in which the media influence attitudes toward business. The major media—large newspapers, television, and, to a lesser extent, radio—are increasingly national in orientation. Their national and international focus, combined with the tendency to emphasize the unusual and sensational—"bad" news— makes it seem to the public that the unusual event is the usual event, that bad news is common. Given such a wide area to cover, such news can always be found, whether it relates to the individual at all. Toxic waste spills are reported wherever they occur, and since the purview of the media is worldwide, the actual number of spills the public hears about is far more than when news was more localized. This gives the public the impression that more things are going wrong than actually are and leads to increased skepticism about the performance of major institutions and leaders.

My intention is not to blame all of society's ills on the media, and the influence of the media on public opinion should not be overdrawn. It does, however, seem reasonable to conclude the following:

1. In the short run, the media can influence public opinion on issues remote from personal experience. This includes but is not limited to matters of business and economic policy.

2. The influence of the media is not random; rather, it reflects its liberal, antibusiness orientation.

3. With more diversity, the direction of influence would not be as uniform.

4. There is an underlying public suspicion that business, particularly big business, is powerful and uses its power in ways contrary to the public interest. This view is reinforced by the media. Without this reinforcement, public suspicion of business would be reduced but not eliminated.

5. The current global scope of the news media in combination with the emphasis on the unusual and sensational story gives the public the impression that more things are wrong than is actually the case. This contributes to the public's reduced faith and confidence in business.

WHAT CAN BE DONE?

Ways to improve overall media coverage of business are difficult to devise. There is certainly no simple solution. In addition to the short-term strategies already discussed, there are some strategies that can be pursued by business that promise to contribute to the long-term improvement of the business climate.

Intellectual Constituency for Business

In Chapter 2 it was argued that there is an intellectual constituency for business emerging within academia. This constituency includes conservative and neo-conservative academics in the social sciences and academics in business whose disciplinary focus includes business and public policy. These conservative and neo-conservative academics emerged as a coherent intellectual force in the late 1960s and early to mid 1970s in reaction against what they felt was a radicalized intellectual establishment. Their major intellectual contribution was to offer a defense of existing values and institutions.

Although policy toward business has become considerably more accommodative since the mid 1970s, the underlying hostility toward business within the new class remains. What business can do to help offset that hostility is to support its small but strategically placed intellectual constituency. This support should include funding for conservative, probusiness research institutes, such as the Heritage Foundation, American Enterprise Institute, and the like. These institutes are extremely important to the policymaking process. They provide financial support and visibility to academics whose views are generally favorable to business and private enterprise, and the fact that such academics are in the public eye lends intellectual respectability and legitimacy to their views among non-academics in the new class. The more conservatively inclined journalists are given an intellectual reference point and source of ideas to support their inclinations.

Business also should exploit its natural relationship with schools of business. The better business schools either are or desire to be accredited by the American Assembly of Collegiate Schools of Business (AACSB). One of the curricular requirements of the AACSB is to have a course or courses devoted to the external environment of business, including such topics as business ethics, business and public policy, and business responsibilities. This requirement has resulted in faculty specialists in the area. Business should encourage this specialization because business students need to be exposed to the ethical and public policy dimensions of business and because research and publication in the area is needed and will benefit business. These academics tend to be conservative and to look for constructive solutions to current business problems. They are a natural complement to the conservative academics in the social sciences. The field of study can be developed by establishing endowed chairs, providing research grants, and emphasizing the importance of such research and teaching to the faculty and dean.

In terms of encouraging an intellectual constituency for business, what is not important is technical research and teaching in the methods and practices of business that does not relate to public policy. Such research ultimately may aid in technical business decision making, but it does nothing to aid business in the debates that are ongoing in the broader intellectual arena.

Economic Education

Another strategy that will help improve the business climate in the long run is economic education. Economic education has long been popular among business leaders. The popularity of economic education in large part stems from the "understand me better and you'll like me more" fallacy. Karl Marx understood how capitalism worked, but he did not like it. Basic attitudes are difficult to change. Still, the public supports private enterprise as a system and may be inclined to do so even more if it had a better understanding of how it operates. It seems reasonable to assume that if people had a better comprehension of how a market economy works, they would understand more readily the implications of complicated economic policies. Such an understanding would limit the influence of the media and result in greater public support for policies beneficial to business.

To be effective, however, economic education programs must be integrated into the regular K–12 curriculum. Business leaders may enjoy going to high schools and telling students about the "real world" of business, but the approach is too sporadic to be effective. Fortunately, in most states there are councils on economic education that develop curriculum materials and show teachers how to use them. (A problem to be overcome in introducing economics into the classroom is that many social studies teachers do not know enough about economics to teach it. These councils often also provide economic education for teachers.)

Such educational efforts, although worthwhile, should be recognized as long-term investments. Creating greater public understanding of economics is a difficult task that can be completed only after a long period of concerted effort.

Excellence in Journalism Awards

A final method of influencing public opinion is based on the model provided by the PKF Financial Writing Achievement Awards. Such awards can be effective because they award responsible journalism. If the stature of the award comes to be highly regarded by journalists, it can influence business reporting in the long run. Certainly, the PKF competition is more effective and less costly than the advocacy advertising of Mobil Oil Company. The key in establishing the legitimacy of such an award is the selection process. The judges in the competition must be highly regarded by journalists, and it must have a significant peer review element in the selection process. The PKF awards meet these criteria and over time should become highly regarded among journalists.

At present, there are only a few highly regarded awards for journalists other than those sponsored by journalists themselves. There is room for probably 15 to 20 national awards and at least an equal number of regional and local awards. If the integrity of these awards can be maintained, they could greatly influence business journalism.

CONCLUDING REMARKS

The message of this book is that business can and ought to manage the media. The assumption is that this management can be accomplished if business people better understand what motivates the media.

The first part of the book was devoted to understanding the attitudes of journalists toward business and their view of the role of the press in society. In the course of that investigation, the differences between business executives and journalists were highlighted. The differences were found to be marked and underscore the need for business to understand better the orientation of the press. A point worth emphasizing is that the views of business and the media are different on some very fundamental issues. The business strategy for dealing with the media should be to recognize and deal with the differences rather than attempting to change the views of journalists.

The second part of the book reviewed a number of examples of business-press interaction. The Seafirst case illustrated the strategy of openness. The Beckman Instruments case represented a policy of closed press relations. Both the Seafirst and Beckman strategies were successful, illustrating the range of available strategies.

The third case involved BKK Corporation and its operation of a hazardous waste disposal site. Like Seafirst, BKK chose to be open with the press; but unlike Seafirst, it also actively attempted to influence press and public opinion. It too was successful. PKF also attempted to influence the press by offering its Financial Writing Achievement Awards. This award program promises to be successful.

As the data and the cases indicate, by being properly informed and devising the appropriate strategy, business can manage the media.

Selected Bibliography

ARTICLES

Banks, Louis. "Why the Media Look Less Fearsome." *Fortune*, October 14, 1985. pp. 206-7.

Benton, M. and J. P. Frazier. "The Agenda-setting Function of the Mass Media at Three Levels of 'Information Holding.' " *Communication Research* 3 (1976): 261-74.

Bernthal, Wilmar F. "The Ideology of the Investigative Reporter." *Business Forum* 9, no. 2 (Spring 1984): 7-9.

"Business Thinks TV Distorts Its Image." *Business Week*, October 18, 1982, p. 26.

Bybee, Carl R. et al. "Mass Communication and Voter Volatility." *Public Opinion Quarterly* 45 (Spring 1981): 69-90.

Chaffee, S. H., L. S. Ward, and L. P. Tipton. "Mass Communications and Political Socialization." *Journalism Quarterly* 47 (1970): 647-59, 666.

Cockburn, Alexander. "When It Comes to Self-Esteem, Journalists Take the Prize." *The Wall Street Journal*, April 19, 1984, p. 33.

"Confidence in Institutions." *The Gallup Report*, July 1985. Report No. 238, pp. 2-12.

Conway, M. Margaret et al. "The News Media in Children's Political Socialization." *Public Opinion Quarterly* 45 (Summer 1981): 164-78.

Cook, Fay Lomax. "Media and Agenda Setting: Effects on the Public, Interest Group Leaders, Policy Makers, and Policy." *Public Opinion Quarterly* 47 (Spring 1983): 16-35.

Erbring, L., E. Goldenberg, and A. Miller. "Front-page News and Real-

World Cues: A New Look at Agenda-Setting by the Media." *American Journal of Political Science* 24 (1980): 16-49.

Evans, Fred J. "The Adversary Ideology of Media Elite." *Los Angeles Business & Economics* 5, no. 2 (Spring 1980): 4-5.

_____. "Business and the Press: Conflicts Over Roles, Fairness." *Public Relations Review* 4 (Winter 1984): 33-42.

_____. "Business: Attacked from Without and Undermined from Within?" *IPRA Review* 7, no. 3 (November 1983): 232.

_____. "The Business-Media Conflict Surveyed." *Business Forum* 9, no. 2 (Spring 1984): 16-23.

_____. "The Business-Media Equation." *Business Forum* 7, no. 2 (Spring 1982): 4.

_____. "The Politics of the Press." *Business Horizons* 10, no. 4 (March/April 1984): 22-29.

Fischman, Joshua. "Views of Network News." *Psychology Today*, July 1986, pp. 16-17.

Greenfield, Meg. "Why We're Still Muckraking." *Newsweek*, March 25, 1985, p. 94.

Heiskell, Andrew. "Andrew Heiskell on the Press." *The Brookings Review* 2, no. 2 (Winter 1983): 24-25.

Herrnstein, R. J. "IQ Testing and the Media." *The Atlantic Monthly* 250, no. 2 (August 1982): 68-74.

Herschensohn, Bruce. "Are the Media Biased?" *KABC*, August 1984, p. 5.

Hess, Stephen. "The Golden Triangle: The Press at the White House, State, and Defense." *The Bookings Review*, Summer 1984, pp. 14-19.

Hunt, Albert R. "Media Bias Is in the Eye of the Beholder." *The Wall Street Journal*, July 23, 1985.

Immerwahr, John. "Public Attitudes Toward Freedom of the Press." *Public Opinion Quarterly* 46 (Summer 1982): 175-94.

Kepplinger, Hans Mathias and Herbert Roth. "Creating a Crisis: German Mass Media and Oil Supply in 1973-74." *Public Opinion Quarterly* 43 (Fall 1979): 285-96.

Kinsley, Michael. "Mobil's Media Master Offers a Corporate Lesson Plan." *The Wall Street Journal*, April 24, 1986, p. 31.

Kolton, Paul, ed. "Business and the Media: Part I. An Uneasy Balance." *Financial Executive*, April 1985, pp. 21-27.

Kowet, Don. "Libel Law No Substitute for Journalistic Standards." *Media Institute Forum* 2, no. 1 (May 1985): 3.

Krugman, Herbert E. and Eugene L. Hartley. "Passive Learning from Television." *Public Opinion Quarterly* 34 (1970): 184-90.

Lambeth, E. "Perceived Influence of the Press on Energy Policy Making." *Journalism Quarterly* 55 (1978): 11-18, 62.

Lichter, S. Robert. "Media Support for Israel: A Survey of Leading Journalists." In William C. Adams, ed. *Television Courage of the Middle East.* Norwood, N.J.: ABLEX, 1981.

Lipman, Joanne. "At the New Yorker, Editor and a Writer Differ on the 'Facts.' " *The Wall Street Journal,* June 18, 1984, p. 1ff.

Maines, Patrick D. "Stocking Toxic Fears." *AEI Journal on Government and Society* (September/October 1985): 48-50.

McCombs, M. and D. L. Shaw. "The Agenda-Setting Functions of the Mass Media." *Public Opinion Quarterly* 36 (1972): 176-87.

McLeod, J. M., L. B. Becker, and J. E. Byrnes. "Another Look at the Agenda-Setting Function of the Press." *Communication Research* 1 (1974): 131-66.

Michener, James A. "Writers Must Tell the Truth—There Are, However, Many Ways to Do So." *Los Angeles Times,* July 1, 1984, p. 1-p.

Mullich, Joe. "The Pressure of the Press." *Pasadena/Altadena Weekly,* January 9-15, 1986, pp. 1-3.

Oliver, William H. "An Executive's View of the Media." *Business Forum* 9, no. 2 (Spring 1984): 13-15.

Powell, Jody. "Press Should Feel a Need to Clean Up Its Own Act." *Los Angeles Times,* April 19, 1982, p. 1.

Ramsey, Bruce. "The Ideology of the Investigative Reporter." *Business Forum* 9, no. 2 (Spring 1984): 10-12.

Reedy, George E. "The Press and the President: There They Go Again." *Columbia Journalism Review* 22, no. 1 (May/June 1983): 35-36.

Robinson, Michael. "Future Television News Research: Beyond Edward J. Epstein." In William Adams and Fay Schreibman, eds., *Television Network News: Issues in Content Research.* Washington, D.C.: George Washington University, School of Public and International Affairs, pp. 197-212.

Rosentiel, Thomas B. "New Yorker Writer Held to Have Altered Facts to Make Stories 'Truer.' " *Los Angeles Times,* June 20, 1984, p. 10.

_____. "Poll Finds Most Americans Believe Press." *Los Angeles Times,* January 16, 1986, p. 1ff.

Rothman, Stanley. "Contorting Scientific Controversies." *Society* 20, no. 5 (July-August 1983): 26-32.

Rothman, Stanley, and S. Robert Lichter. "Are Journalists a New Class?" *Business Forum* 8, no. 2 (Spring 1983): 12-17.

_____. "How Liberal are Bureaucrats?" *AEI Journal on Government and Society* (November/December 1983): 16-22.

_____. "Media Versus Business." *Current*, January 1983, pp. 37-45.

_____. "The Nuclear Energy Debate: Scientists, The Media and the Public." *Public Opinion* (August/September 1982): 47-52.

_____. "What Are Movie Makers Made Of?" *Public Opinion* 6, no. 6 (December/January 1984): 14-18.

Schneider, William and I. A. Lewis. "Views on the News." *Public Opinion* 8, no. 4 (August/September 1985): 6-11ff.

Seligman, Daniel. "Who Could Be Fairer than Us?" *Fortune*, January 6, 1986.

Shaw, David. "Anonymity Questioned: 'Sources Said': Who Are They?" *Los Angeles Times*, November 17, 1982, p. 1ff.

_____. "Media: High Ratings are Tempered." *Los Angeles Times*, August 12, 1985, p. 1ff.

_____. "Plagiarism: A Taint in Journalism." *Los Angeles Times*, July 5, 1984, p. 1ff.

Siddons, Patrick. "Business and Journalism: Bedfellows or Mortal Enemies?" *Contents* (September/October 1985): 3-7.

Tuchman, Gaye. "Objectivity as Strategic Ritual: An Examination of Newsmen's Notion of Objectivity." *American Journal of Sociology* 77 (January 1972): 660-79.

Watson, George. "Corporate Press Relations: Journalists Sound Off." *Media Institute Forum* 2, no. 2 (Fall 1985): 1ff.

Wattenberg, Martin P. "From Parties to Candidates: Examining the Role of the Media." *Public Opinion Quarterly* 46 (Summer 1982): 217-27.

Weaver, Paul. "Is Television News Biased?" *The Public Interest* 26 (Winter 1972): 57-74.

Welles, Chris. "The Craft of Business Reporting." *Folio*, May 1982, pp. 94-101.

Will, George F. "TV News Goes for Emotions, Not Minds." *Los Angeles Times*, October 2, 1982, p. 3.

Winship, Thomas. "Shop Talk at Thirty." *Editor & Publisher*, December 29, 1984, pp. 30-31.

Young, Lewis H. "Business and the Media: Part II. A Distorted Image?" *Financial Executive*, April 1985, pp. 29-32.

BOOKS

Aronoff, Craig E. *Business and the Media*. Santa Monica: Goodyear, 1979.

Bethell, Tom. *Television Evening News Covers Inflation: 1978-79*. Washington, D.C.: The Media Institute, 1980.

Bell, Daniel. *The Cultural Contradictions of Capitalism.* New York: Basic Books, 1976.

Braestrup, Peter. *Big Story: How the American Press and Television Reported and Interpreted the Crisis of Tet 1968 in Vietnam and Washington,* 2 vols. Boulder, Colo.: Westview Press, 1977.

Bruce-Briggs, B., ed. *The New Class.* New Jersey: Transaction Books, 1979.

Drayer, Michael. *Issues in Communication.* Washington, D.C.: The Media Institute, 1985.

Hess, Stephen. *The Washington Reporter.* Washington, D.C.: The Brookings Institution, 1981.

Hofstetter, Richard. *Bias in the News.* Columbus: Ohio State University Press, 1971.

_____. *Bias in the News: Network Television Coverage of the 1972 Election Campaign.* Columbus: Ohio State University Press, 1976.

Johnstone, J. W., Edward J. Slawski, and William Bowman. *The News People.* Bloomington: University of Illinois Press, 1976.

Klapper, Joseph T. *The Effects of Mass Communications.* New York: Free Press, 1960.

Kristol, Irving. *Reflections of a Neoconservative.* New York: Basic Books, 1983.

Lawler, Philip F. *Sweet Talk.* Washington, D.C.: The Media Institute, 1986.

Lichter, Linda S. and S. Robert Lichter. *Prime Time Crime.* Washington, D.C.: The Media Institute, 1983.

Lipset, Seymour Martin. *The Third Century.* Stanford, Calif.: Hoover Institute Press, 1979.

MacDougall, A. Kent. *Ninety Seconds to Tell It All.* Homewood: Dow Jones-Irwin, 1981.

Maines, Patrick D. *TV News Covers the Budget Debate.* Washington, D.C.: The Media Institute, 1986.

Patterson, Thomas and Robert McClure. *The Unseeing Eye: The Myth of Television Power in National Politics.* New York: G. P. Putnam's Sons, 1976.

Rivers, William. *The Opinionmakers.* Boston: Little, Brown, 1965.

Rossie, Charles M., Jr., ed. *Media Resource Guide,* 4th ed. Los Angeles: FACS, 1985.

Schmertz, Herbert. *The Press and the Public.* Remarks Before Annual Review Meeting of Gannett News Service, Washington, D.C., December 13, 1983.

Shaw, D. L. and M. E. McCombs, eds. *The Emergence of American Political Issues: The Agenda-Setting Function of the Press.* St. Paul: West, 1977.

Simon, Raymond. *Publicity and Public Relations Worktex*, 5th ed. Columbus: Grid Publishing, 1979.

Simons, Howard and Joseph A. Califano, Jr., eds. *The Media and Business*. New York: Vintage Books, 1979.

Stein, Ben. *The View from Sunset Boulevard*. New York: Basic Books, 1979.

Tedone, David. *Practical Publicity*. Boston: The Harvard Common Press, 1983.

Theberge, Leonard J., ed. *TV Coverage of the Oil Crisis: How Well Was the Public Served?* Washington, D.C.: The Media Institute, 1982.

Wattenberg, Ben J. *The Good News Is the Bad News Is Wrong*. New York: Simon and Schuster, 1984.

Index

About the Author

FRED J. EVANS, Associate Dean of Fiscal Affairs at the School of Business and Economics, California State University, Los Angeles, is the Executive Editor of *Business Forum*. His longstanding interest in business-media relations began with his experiences as Public Affairs Officer at Seattle-First National Bank. He has published widely in professional journals as diverse as the *Journal of Politics* and *Business*.